PRAISE FOR GENE GRIESSMAN'S WORK

"Gene Griessman has done it again—with yet another fast-moving, unexpected, captivating riff on the history we thought we knew. This book sheds new light on what may be the most meaningful presidential relationship that has ever existed across time."

– Harold Holzer, author of *Emancipating Lincoln* and chairman of The Lincoln Bicentennial Foundation

"Thousands have written about Lincoln, but few understand him. Lincoln is difficult to understand. Gene Griessman understands him. He has plumbed his soul."

– Wayne C. Temple, Lincoln scholar and author of *Abraham Lincoln: From Skeptic to Prophet*

"Prof. Griessman has done a superb job. His book is outstanding. Not only does Griessman give us Lincoln quotes, but he also weaves each one into a little jewel of an essay on that particular subject. If a reader peruses a chapter a week, he or she will have a year's worth of inspiration."

– Review by Wayne C. Temple of *The Words Lincoln Lived By* for *The Lincoln Herald*

"Griessman has done a masterful service in rendering Lincoln's colossal wisdom of leadership to contemporary leaders and managers. It's uncanny everything written about leadership today that is anything that's significant— was spoken or written by Lincoln at least 130 years ago. And Griessman illuminates Lincoln's brilliance to all of us."

– Warren Bennis, Distinguished Professor of Business Administration, University of Southern California and author of *Organizing Genius*

"First rate. Lincoln's thoughts on just about anything are compelling, and here, they are artfully broken down into various categories, each brief and brisk. *The Words Lincoln Lived By* makes the quality of his greatness accessible to a wide variety of readers."

– Steve Forbes, Editor-in-Chief, *Forbes*

"Abraham Lincoln's words prove to be timeless in this engaging and insightful work. *Lincoln Speaks to Leaders* is an important read for all those who wish to improve their leadership skills."

– Donald T. Phillips, author of *Lincoln on Leadership*

"Lincoln on Communication is one of the very best videos/DVDs ever made. It's a classic like *Gone With The Wind*. I show it in many of my seminars. Everyone loves it."

– Brad McRae, author of
The Seven Strategies of Master Presenters

"*Lincoln on Communication* is a compelling and memorable educational experience and a joy to watch and listen to. I show this peerless presentation to every class I teach and I always look forward to seeing it again. It is not unusual for students to give it a standing ovation."

– Bill Funchion, Waubonsee Community College,
Sugar Grove, Illinois

ADDITIONAL TITLES BY GENE GRIESSMAN

Minorities

The Achievement Factors

Lessons from Legends

Diversity: Challenges and Opportunities

The Southern Mystique: Technology and Human Values in a Changing Region
Co-author: W. David Lewis

Time Tactics of Very Successful People

The Words Lincoln Lived By

Lincoln Speaks to Leaders
Co-authors Pat Williams and Peggy Matthews Rose

99 Ways to Get More Out Of Every Day

The Path to High Achievement

The Inspirational Words of Abraham Lincoln

Lincoln's Wisdom

Lincoln on Communication

LINCOLN AND OBAMA

LINCOLN
AND OBAMA

GENE GRIESSMAN
Winner of the Benjamin Franklin Award

An Achievement Digest Book

***BOOK*LOGIX®

*BOOK*LOGIX®
Alpharetta, Georgia

ISBN: 978-1-61005-234-4

Library of Congress Control Number: 2012915413

Printed in the United States of America

∞This paper meets the requirements of ANSI/NISO Z39.48-1992 (Permanence of Paper)

Illustrator: Sergey Kondratenko

A nation that does not know its past is ignorant.
Teach it.
A nation that lives in its past is asleep.
Awaken it.
A nation that does not learn from its past is in danger.
Warn it.

– Gene Griessman

CONTENTS

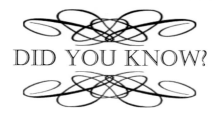

DID YOU KNOW?

Both are lawyers.

Both serve in the Illinois legislature and represent Illinois in Congress, but neither is born in Illinois.

Both gain national attention through big speeches—Lincoln at the Cooper Institute and Obama as keynote speaker at the Democratic National Convention.

There is an economic collapse of international proportions just before each presidency.

Neither Lincoln nor Obama ever carry the Deep South or Texas.

Lincoln and Obama are the only two politicians ever to be elected president who outspokenly oppose an American war. Lincoln opposes the Mexican War, and Obama, the Iraq War.

Both are talented athletes. Lincoln, a wrestler, and Obama, a basketball player.

Both love poetry and write poems in their youth.

Both are called dictators. Kentucky senator Rand Paul calls Obama "King Obama;" Lincoln was often called "King Abraham" by Confederates.

Both are objects of intense love and hatred as well as assassination threats.

Both succeed presidents—James Buchanan and George W. Bush—who suffer a dramatic drop in popularity before they leave office.

Both criticize controversial Supreme Court decisions.

Both are loved abroad.

Both adopt a cautious foreign policy.

Both are sympathetic toward immigrants.

Both contend with states' rights advocates.

Both are called unpatriotic, divisive and extreme.

Both advocate women's issues.

Both have top generals who are authors of celebrated books on military strategy—for Lincoln, General Henry Halleck, and for Obama, General David Petraeus.

Both are obscure politicians who overtake the frontrunner of the party. In each case, the frontrunner is a New York Senator.

Both win second terms by a huge electoral vote margin. Lincoln gets 55% of the popular vote and Obama 50.79%.

ACHIEVEMENT   www.lincolnandobama.com

Get your own digital download of this poster at www.lincolnandobama.com

HISTORY AND YOU

"The only new thing in the world is the history you don't know."

– Harry Truman

Why should you care, why should anybody care, if there are parallels and similarities between Abraham Lincoln and Barack Obama?

You care if you're interested in your personal success.

You will learn how high achievers become high achievers. This is a story not just about two presidents, but two entire casts of high achievers. Not one individual is a cipher.

Success has its own set of rules. You will learn some of those rules here. High achievers learn to play to their strengths, not their weaknesses. High achievers learn to recognize opportunities when they come their way, and seize them. High achievers become very good at what they do; they learn how to learn. High achievers focus. High achievers are resilient, persistent.

It is a common experience of all high achievers, not just presidents, to find that staying aloft is as difficult as getting aloft. Often more difficult.

You will see all of this happening in these stories. They can be treated like case studies that students analyze in schools of business.

You will also get a better grasp of what history really is. That it's not just a checklist of dates and names and battles. It is a story of men, women, and children making choices that determine everything that happens thereafter—to them and to those around them. Here is the story of two men who make high-stakes choices, and life is never again the same.

In addition, these parallel stories will help you understand how American government really works. If you're an American, you owe that to yourself.

Interestingly, in these stories you will meet individuals who expect too much of the president, blame him more than they should, ridicule him too often, hate him too much.

We love Lincoln now, but in his own time he was the target of more derision and pure hatred than perhaps any president ever.

Finally, reading about Lincoln and Obama in tandem will give you a different perspective on *both* presidents. No longer will you think that just Lincoln or just Obama behave a certain way. You will understand that every individual who resides in the White House is controlled by rules and constraints that he does not create. But the best ones say, "I will do the best I can, so help me God."

History Repeats Itself

Some of the repetition is random and coincidental, has no significance, no meaning.

But some of history's repetition *is* meaningful. We live in a cause-and-effect universe. The same cause produces the same effects over and over again.

Lincoln was aware of this. "There were no accidents in his philosophy," Lincoln's partner Billy Herndon wrote. "Every effect had its cause." As soon as Lincoln had a sense of which way events were moving, he positioned himself so to take advantage of the movement," his friend Leonard Swett observed: "His tactics were to get himself in the right place, and remain there still, until events would find him in that place."

Social scientists recognize that every situation has a limited number of options–in other words, there are *situational imperatives*. What makes the difference in history is which option is chosen.

Shakespeare understood this. That's why we still read him. We watch his characters consider their options, wrestle with their choices, make their decisions.

Déjà Vu

Barack Obama has an important part in one of the uncanny repetitions in American history.

Here's the story. Lincoln and Obama, separated by 150 years, overtake the front-runner and presumed nominee of their respective parties. They both win the nomination after a nasty, hard-fought struggle.

The favorites that Lincoln and Obama overtake are much better known than they are, and each of them is a US senator from the state of New York.

Supporters of both the senators are incredulous, resentful, and angry. Some vow that they will vote for another candidate. But most go along with the nominee for the good of their party. The presidents-elect entreat the senators to become secretary of state. After much wooing, the senators accept. Each becomes an outstanding secretary of state. Each becomes a friendly supporter of the president.

Now a few details…

It's 1860. Abraham Lincoln, an Illinois lawyer and one-term congressman, has just been nominated as the Republican candidate for president. He has practically no national reputation and no executive experience.

The front-runner William Seward is a refined, college-educated, well-traveled man. He has served as governor of New York, and is now a US senator. Because he is the most prominent politician from the most populous state in the nation, most people naturally assume that Seward is the man to talk to about all things Republican. Few would think to contact a small-town lawyer named Lincoln in faraway Springfield, Illinois. The contrast between the two is stark—almost laughable.

But Seward has powerful enemies who despise him. He is too extreme, too much an abolitionist to carry the whole country. His enemies plot against him, look for somebody who can run against him, someone who can beat him. Maybe an unknown without baggage. They settle on Lincoln, give him favorable publicity, and organize a big speech in New York City in the large auditorium of Cooper Institute. Lincoln's speech exceeds every expectation. Horace Greeley, who dislikes Seward, puffs Lincoln in his newspaper, the *New York Tribune*. Lincoln begins to get national name-recognition, but still not nearly as much as Seward.

The Republicans hold their convention in Chicago. Lincoln doesn't attend. Lincoln's people tell him to leave matters to them. They shrewdly outmaneuver Seward's supporters. The voting begins. Seward doesn't clinch victory on the first ballot. Lincoln overtakes Seward, passes him on the third ballot. Seward's people yell foul. They claim Lincoln's supporters packed the huge convention hall known as the Wigwam with bogus tickets. They accuse Lincoln's people of cutting unseemly deals. But it doesn't matter. Lincoln is the party nominee. Seward is stunned. Humiliated. Feels unappreciated, betrayed. Goes back home to New York to grieve.

Lincoln has no personal grudge against Seward. Never has carried grudges. Is as surprised as anybody else at his victory. Is a little embarrassed by it, actually, but pleased. Lincoln is after all an ambitious man.

President-elect Lincoln knows he must have a strong cabinet, needs to surround himself with people who know more than he does, who can do what he can't.

There ensues a ballet between Seward and Lincoln. They circle one another. Lincoln needs to make sure there aren't two presidents in the White House. Seward is a flirt. He will. He won't. He might. He wants to know what position is being offered. Secretary of state? Hearing that it is, he replies, "Well, maybe, that is if Mr. Chase, governor of Ohio, is not in your cabinet. You know that I don't like Mr. Chase. You've asked Salmon Chase to be secretary of Treasury? Let me think about it. Well, all right, I'll do it."

Lincoln thinks he has a deal. When he arrives in Washington just prior to his inauguration, Seward is the first man to meet him. The two are together constantly. Seward introduces Lincoln to everybody who matters. Personally accompanies him most places. Seward is the insider, Lincoln the outsider.

Lincoln takes Seward into his confidence about his big speech. Seward is flattered. Makes many recommendations, some very good. Lincoln is grateful.
Then, like a thunderbolt, literally hours before the inauguration, comes this message from Seward: "Circumstances which have occurred since I expressed to you in December last my willingness to accept the office of Secretary of State, seem to me to render it my duty to ask leave to withdraw that consent."

It seems Seward has learned that Lincoln has asked Chase to be in the cabinet after all. Lincoln stands his ground, says to his secretaries, "I can't afford to let Seward take the first trick."

He gives Seward an ultimatum: come on board with the people I've chosen, or back out, and hurt me, hurt the party, and hurt your own reputation.

Seward does not take the first trick.

Once on board, Seward lets it be known that he intends to be an American version of a prime minister. Lincoln will serve in a more or less honorary capacity.

Seward lets journalists and key politicians know that they can come to him if they want to get insider information about the big decisions, and that includes dealing with the Fort Sumter situation.

Seward underestimates Lincoln. The president senses what Seward is up to. He tells Mary. She knows how shrewd and tough Lincoln is.

Seward guesses wrong about Fort Sumter. Meddles with a sensitive order involving the USS *Powhatan*, a side-wheel steam frigate in the United States Navy. There's much confusion, much embarrassment.

Seward settles down. Learns to appreciate and respect Lincoln's talents. Realizes their talents complement one another.

The two become friends to the end. Lincoln is shot in Ford's Theatre. At almost the same hour, Seward is attacked in his home by an assassin. This is part of the plot that John Wilkes Booth has hatched, and it is going according to plan.

Seward is in bed when the attack occurs, recovering from a nearly fatal carriage accident nine days earlier.

Seward's son Fred remembers later that a tall, well-dressed man had presented himself at the door. He was actually Lewis Powell, who had been meeting in secret with John Wilkes Booth. Powell told the servant who answered the bell that he had some medicine for Mr. Seward, and had been instructed by his physician to deliver it in person.

Powell pushes by Seward's son. Fred tries to stop the intruder at the stair landing. Powell draws a Navy revolver, and fires at the boy. The pistol misfires. Powell then uses the pistol as a club, and brings it down on Fred's head, knocking him unconscious.

Powell rushes up the stairs and into the bedroom, sticks a Bowie knife into Seward's neck and face, and severs his cheek so badly that it flaps loose on his neck. When the doctor arrives, Seward is barely alive. All this happens around 10:15 p.m. Lincoln is assassinated at 10:30.

Seward lies unconscious for days, then rouses. Asks about Lincoln. Gets an evasive answer. Drifts back into semi-consciousness. Asks about Lincoln again. Gets another evasive answer. Seward then says, "The president is dead, isn't he? How do I know? If Lincoln were alive, he would be here."

Seward recovers, and he becomes President Andrew Johnson's secretary of state. He recommends purchasing Alaska. In 1867, a deal is struck with Russia for $7.2 million. The purchase is mocked as "Seward's ice box," "Seward's folly." Gold is discovered in the Klondike thirty years later, and five years later, oil. People have stopped calling it a folly. A town in Alaska is named Seward.

Now it's 2008. A great many Democrats believe Hillary Clinton will become America's first woman president. She certainly has the credentials. A lawyer like Seward, a senator from New York, she has lived in the White House as First Lady for eight years. She has met face-to-face with the movers and shakers of the earth. By all accounts, she can dazzle with her intelligence.

When Obama is mentioned as a contender, he is so far behind it is ludicrous. In 2007, pollsters ask, "Who has the best chance of winning, Hillary Clinton or Obama?" The poll results are 71 percent to 26 percent.

Some say Hillary is actually smarter than Bill, which is saying a lot. Bill's intelligence is more expansive and wide-ranging than hers. She is more focused, more controlled. Hillary is not as comfortable with people as he is. Maybe nobody is. His social intelligence is off the chart, way into genius territory. Both Clintons have big egos, big ambitions.

But, like William Seward, Hillary Clinton has a lot of political baggage and a lot of enemies. John Heilemann and Mark Halperin in *Game Change* call her "the *bête noir* of the Republican Right." Her negative ratings are described as "perilously high."

Obama manages to beat Clinton after hard-fought primary battles. Clinton comes close, tantalizingly close to getting the nomination, just like Seward did. Of the 36 million votes cast, only 150,000 votes separate the two. And just like Seward's supporters, many are angry, and feel disaffected when Hillary Clinton loses. *The Wall Street Journal* conducts a poll just after Obama wins. About half of Clinton's supporters say they will support Obama. Many are undecided. Some say they will stay home election day. And one in five of her supporters say they will vote for the candidate of the other party, John McCain.

Obama lets it be known in his inner circle that he would not rule out Hillary for a top cabinet post. Tells them he admires a lot of her qualities.

There's a strong push back to the Hillary Clinton idea. Several of Obama's closest campaign advisors think she will pursue her own agenda, will undermine Obama's, will be a constant headache.

If there is a conscious attempt to construct a Lincoln and Seward redux, Obama's top advisors seem not to know about it.

Obama's wooing of Hillary has the same feel as Lincoln's courtship of Seward. It's 1860 all over again. The words are almost the same. Are they reading a script?

No, I'm not interested. Not really, but maybe. No, I don't think I'm interested, but I am willing to meet with you and talk about it. No, I've thought it over, and the answer is still no. But I'm flattered. I'm planning a press conference to announce that I'm going to continue to serve in Congress, where I can serve my country best. You really want me that much. Well, okay. I'll do it.

Amateur Presidents

There are three famous American presidents who are called "amateurs," or words to that effect, by their critics: *Lincoln, Kennedy, and Obama.* There are all sorts of parallels among these three presidents. The ones between Lincoln and JFK are rather well-known.

Here are a few of them...One. Lincoln is elected president in 1860, JFK in 1960. Two. Both are nominated unsuccessfully for the vice presidency. Lincoln in 1856, JFK in 1956. Three. Both lose sons in the White House. Lincoln's son is named Willie, Kennedy's son is named Patrick. Four. Both presidents are assassinated on a Friday, each seated beside his wife. Five. There are seven letters in the name Lincoln; seven in the name Kennedy. Six. Both assassins use all three names. Seven. There are fifteen letters in John Wilkes Booth. There are fifteen letters in Lee Harvey Oswald. Eight. Both presidents' wives can speak French. Nine. Both presidents are succeeded by Democrats named Johnson—Andrew Johnson and Lyndon Johnson. Ten. Andrew Johnson is born in 1808, and Lyndon Johnson is born in 1908.

There are more parallels, many in fact.

Obama's Guiding Star

It's a freezing cold day in Springfield, Illinois, so wintry they place a heating device in the base of the speaker's lectern. So wintry the high this day is 7 degrees. Barack Obama, hatless and clad in a long overcoat, stands outside the Old State Capital Building where Lincoln once stood a century and a half earlier.

It's Saturday, February 10, 2007, just two days shy of Lincoln's birthday. Only three years have passed since Obama was still an Illinois state senator in Springfield. Now he is announcing his intention to become president of the United States. He acknowledges how audacious this is, saying he hopes to wear the mantle of a president who's on Mt. Rushmore. Says his inexperience in Washington is an asset: "I know that I haven't spent a lot of time learning the ways of Washington. But I've been there long enough to know that the ways of Washington must change."

But he is taken seriously. A shivering crowd gathers as close to Obama as possible. Seventeen thousand of them. Every hotel and motel in town has been sold out for days.

Obama is versed in Lincoln history; he studies Doris Kearns Goodwin's *Team of Rivals*, quotes from it, decides to run his first and second campaigns in Illinois, "The Land of Lincoln."

When he is sworn in, Obama asks to use the same Bible that was used for the same purpose at Lincoln's inauguration. No previous president has used the Lincoln Bible. The Library of Congress loans it from its collection.

Every day he's in the Oval Office, Obama looks at George Henry Story's portrait of Lincoln. Above a bust of Martin Luther King, Jr. is an original copy of the Emancipation Proclamation—signed by Lincoln.

Obama contributes a short essay to *The Atlantic* magazine in July 2012. In it he says: "Lincoln is a president I turn to often. From time to time, I'll walk over to the Lincoln Bedroom and reread the handwritten Gettysburg Address encased in glass, or reflect on the Emancipation Proclamation, which hangs in the Oval Office, or pull a volume of his writings from the library in search of lessons to draw."

Obama invokes Lincoln's name to lusty cheers at a speech in Florida. He's talking about his stimulus program. He states that Lincoln believed in education…tells them about the Morrill Act, which Lincoln signed early in the Civil War. Obama tells them it created the land grant colleges. Schools like Michigan State and Kansas State. "Lincoln believed in building up America's infrastructure," he says, "just like I do." In the middle of the Civil War, Obama tells the crowd in that distinctive cadence of his, the transcontinental railroad begins; now we can rebuild our decaying bridges, tunnels, and highways. This, Obama says, to much cheering and applause.

He can give one heck of a speech, work a crowd. Even Obama's harshest critics admit that.

But what Obama says in Florida is not just rhetoric, not just easy comparisons.

What Obama says is true. All that did happen during Lincoln's administration. During very dark days of the war, when Union forces were losing more battles than they were winning, great schools were begun, and the transcontinental railroad was started. Lincoln is thinking about more than just winning the war. Lincoln is thinking about the larger future. Lincoln is that kind of man.

As a former Whig, Lincoln believes in what politicians in his day called "internal improvements." Being for internal improvements is one of the big differentiators between the Whigs and Andrew Jackson Democrats who believed in small government.

Lincoln is a president who never goes to college, or even high school, or even middle school, just about one year in what they called "ABC" schools. But Lincoln believes in public education. The land-grant colleges are right down his alley because they give common folk—the "industrial classes," like farmers and mechanics and merchants and engineers and architects—a chance to get a college education.

The Morrill Act specifies that these new colleges, which will be called A&M, for agriculture and mechanical, will be funded by the sale of federal lands. That's why they're called "land grant" schools.

Those land grant schools begin to transform American agriculture from a hit-or-miss, primitive enterprise into an efficient, scientific behemoth that today produces billions of dollars in exports. Not a bad return on a Lincoln-administration investment.

In the Same Category?

Q: "Are you putting Obama in the same category with Lincoln?"

A: Nobody is in the same category with Lincoln except George Washington. But, the similarities and parallels are uncanny."

– Gene Griessman interview,
The Small Business Advocate, 2012

You may hate Obama or love him. But there are striking similarities between Lincoln, Number 16, and Obama,

Number 44. Almost as striking as the ones you've heard between Lincoln and Kennedy.

The parallels and similarities between Lincoln and Obama, when taken one by one, are not as mysterious as those between Lincoln and Kennedy.

Some are superficial. They both are tall. They both have big ears. Some are predictable. What you might expect when two obscure American lawyer-politicians aspire to high national office. But taken together, the parallels and similarities are impressive.

Practically everything negative that is said about Lincoln is said about Obama. It's remarkable how similar the criticisms are. Virtually word-for-word. Both presidents evoke intense love and intense hatred.

> Americans love Lincoln today, but in his day, millions despised him. Lincoln did not get on Mount Rushmore right away.

"I can't understand the visceral reaction to Obama—the hatred," an insurance salesman in Georgia tells me. "If the man was mean-spirited, I could understand it, but he's not." Robert English, a television producer in Upstate New York tells me, "If Obama were a white Republican, we'd be naming streets and airports after him."

Dissimilarities

Some individuals in history and some historical events are alike. The French Revolution, the American Revolution and the Russian Revolution have parallels. But no two or three revolutions or individuals are identical.

Before getting into the similarities between Lincoln and Obama, here are some ways that they are not alike, some of them pretty obvious. Lincoln is white, Obama is not. Lincoln goes to school about one year; Obama has a college degree and a law degree. Lincoln's children are boys, Obama's are girls. Obama can sing, Lincoln can't.

I.
BIOGRAPHICAL TOUCHSTONES

Biographies are but the clothes and buttons of the man. The biography of the man himself cannot be written.

– Mark Twain

BIOGRAPHICAL TOUCHSTONES

Humble Origins

Neither Lincoln nor Obama come from great wealth like George Washington, Franklin Delano Roosevelt, or George W. Bush. They grow up in obscurity—on the frontier; in Hawaii and Indonesia.

Lincoln

Here is how Lincoln describes his origins: "It is a great piece of folly to attempt to make anything out of my early life. It can be condensed into a simple sentence, and that sentence you will find in Gray's Elegy—'the short and simple annals of the Poor.'[1] That's my life, and that's all you or anyone else can make out of it." And there's also: "I was a friendless, uneducated, penniless boy."

He is born in Kentucky, not in the beautiful town of Lexington, but miles away, deep in the forest. Lincoln's family moves to Indiana when he is just a boy.

Lincoln tells in a campaign biography what it is like to grow up on the frontier on the very outskirts of civilization:

> We reached our new home [in Indiana] about the time the state came into the Union. It was a wild region, with many bears and other wild animals still in the woods. There I grew up. There were some schools, so called; but no qualification was ever required of a teacher beyond

---

[1] From the poem "Elegy Written in a Country Church-Yard" by Thomas Gray.

3

'readin, writin, and cipherin' to the Rule of Three. If a straggler supposed to understand Latin happened to sojourn in the neighborhood, he was looked upon as a wizard [sic]. There was absolutely nothing to excite ambition for education. Of course when I came of age I did not know much. Still somehow, I could read, write and cipher to the Rule of Three; but that was all. I have not been to school since. The little advance I now have upon this store of education, I have picked up from time to time under the pressure of necessity.

From rural Indiana, Lincoln moves with his family to Illinois. He is twenty-one years old. He helps his family build a log cabin about ten miles from Decatur, then ventures out on his own. When he is twenty-two years old, he settles in New Salem, Illinois. It is a tiny place, with never more than 300 people residing in it.

Six years later, Lincoln moves to Springfield. He resides there— except for two years when he lives in Washington while a Congressman—until he is elected president.

Looking back, Lincoln says:

I am not ashamed to confess that twenty-five years ago I was a hired laborer, mauling rails, at work on [a] flatboat—just what might happen to any poor man's son. I want every man to have the chance, and I believe a black man is entitled to it—in which he can better his condition—when he may look forward and hope to be a hired laborer this year and the next, work for himself afterwards, and finally to hire men to work for him. That is the true system.

Not one of the places where Lincoln resides is a great center of power. Springfield is the state capital, and it attracts talented individuals who become national leaders. But in 1860 its

4

population has grown to just 16,000 inhabitants. Chicago's population, by contrast, has already reached 109,000 in 1860. Lincoln is called a small-town lawyer.

Note: You'll find the story of how Lincoln became a lawyer in "II. Remarkable Career Paths."

Obama

Obama's mother's family is not poor, but it certainly is not rich.

He tells a journalist about taking a vacation when he is eleven years old. They travelled on a Greyhound bus, stayed at Howard Johnson's. He says: "If there was any kind of swimming pool, it didn't matter how big it was. We got ice for the room in a plastic bucket at an ice machine."

As he shares these memories, Obama is connecting with a crowd of supporters. He continues: "You know what that's like," and they nod, because they have all stayed in motels that don't have room service.

Obama remembers his youth: "My mother was on food stamps while she was getting her Ph.D."

Obama lives first in Hawaii. When he is a baby, he lives for a few months in Seattle, where his mother is enrolled at the University of Washington. They return to Honolulu, and live there from 1983 until 1987. That year they move to Jakarta, Indonesia, to live with his stepfather. Four years later, Obama returns to Hawaii where he remains until he graduates from high school. Honolulu and Jakarta (which Obama leaves when he finishes the fourth grade) are certainly important cities, but it is a stretch to say that either place is a Washington or a New York, a London or a Paris.

Legitimacy

There are birth questions about both presidents.

Lincoln

A docent is showing a group of visitors though an antebellum mansion in the Deep South. "Look at that portrait of Jefferson Davis," she says. "Who does it look like?" Somebody in the group answers, "Abraham Lincoln." "Right," says the docent. "Now I'm not accusing anybody of anything, but the Lincoln family and the Davis family lived just ninety miles apart in Kentucky. And Jeff Davis's father did travel a good bit."

Even in the twenty-first century there are still people, mainly in the South, who believe that Abraham Lincoln and Jefferson Davis had the same biological father.

Lincoln historians dismiss the Lincoln-Jefferson Davis rumor as fanciful speculation, but the rumor refuses to die.

Obama

The questions about Lincoln's birth are whispered, and they are mainly confined to books that not many people read. But questions about Obama's birth are the subject of mass-circulation books, newspaper articles, blogs, emails, TV features, debates in Congress.

The people who say Obama's presidency is illegitimate have come to be known as "birthers." Donald Trump, who briefly flirted with a presidential run, gets national attention for his birther views, almost whenever he chooses to raise the question.

According to the birthers, Obama's presidency is illegitimate because he was born in Kenya, and not in the United States. Many birthers seem not to know, or care, that the Constitution says nothing about being *born* in the United States. The

Constitution's words are "natural born" citizen (as opposed to "naturalized" citizen).

These words mean that even if, for the sake of argument, Obama's Hawaiian birth certificate is not genuine, Obama is still a natural born American citizen. Why? Because his mother is a natural born American citizen.

Every year, American women—married and unmarried—give birth to sons and daughters in Germany and Japan and the Netherlands and wherever. Their babies are Americans citizens because the mothers are.

II.
REMARKABLE CAREER PATHS

It is not the critic who counts: not the man who points out how the strong man stumbles or where the doer of deeds could have done better. The credit belongs to the man who is actually in the arena, whose face is marred by dust and sweat and blood, who strives valiantly, who errs and comes up short again and again, because there is no effort without error or shortcoming, but who knows the great enthusiasms, the great devotions, who spends himself for a worthy cause; who, at the best, knows, in the end, the triumph of high achievement, and who, at the worst, if he fails, at least he fails while daring greatly, so that his place shall never be with those cold and timid souls who knew neither victory nor defeat.

– Theodore Roosevelt

REMARKABLE CAREER PATHS

Careers, like symphonies, cannot be fully evaluated until they are finished. In a great symphony, there are motifs and themes in the overture that will be repeated later. Some you will hear only once. In the early careers of Lincoln and Obama, there are motifs—little experiments—that occur once or twice, while others evolve into powerful themes that are developed throughout their lives.

Both Are Lawyers

People generally think of Lincoln and Obama primarily as politicians and as presidents, not as lawyers. But the law plays a huge role in their careers.

> The law is a way of thinking. It is a particular way of looking at situations, with its own logic for understanding and interpreting what is known. It requires the detachment necessary to step back from a case in order to coolly examine it on its merits.

Their experience with the law prepares them for the challenges of the presidency. Obviously it gives them experience writing and speaking. It teaches them discipline. Lawyers are, after all, servants of the clock and the calendar. There are deadlines to meet, and documents must be filed and written just so.

Years before Lincoln or Obama pick up their first law book, Edmund Burke says, "The study of law renders men acute, inquisitive, dexterous, prompt in attack, ready in defense, full of resources. No other profession is more closely connected with actual life than the law. It concerns the highest of all temporal interests of man—property, reputation, the peace of all families, the arbitrations and peace of nations, liberty, life, even the very foundations of society."

Lincoln

When Lincoln looks back on his early years, he speaks of himself as a floating piece of driftwood. He drifts from one job to the next. He is a bargeman and a day laborer, a surveyor and a postmaster, a rail-splitter and a clerk in a store.

Then something happens that changes all that. He comes upon a copy of William Blackstone's *Commentaries on the Laws of England*, and begins to study.

Lincoln later will write, "The more I read, the more intensely interested I became. Never in my whole life was my mind so thoroughly absorbed. I read until I devoured them."

His life is never again the same. He has an aim now, a sense of purpose. It is an existential experience. Lincoln has found his calling.

An old acquaintance drops by the store in New Salem where Lincoln works, and finds Lincoln poring over a book. He asks Lincoln what he's reading. "I ain't reading," Lincoln answers. "I'm studying." "Great God a'mighty," the man says. Lincoln, of all people, the fellow who is best known in the village as an idler, a story-teller.

There are no lawyers in New Salem, so Lincoln begins to use a form book to help his neighbors with wills and deeds and simple contracts. Lincoln does it without charge. He asks lawyer John Todd Stuart, someone he got to know during the Black Hawk

War, to lend him some law books. Stuart, by the way, is a cousin of Mary Todd, Lincoln's future wife. Before long, Stuart and Lincoln are partners.

In those days it is fairly simple to become a lawyer. The biggest hurdle is learning enough law to get three lawyers to recommend you. Lincoln does that, and begins his practice.

After a while Lincoln makes a career move. He changes partners. Lincoln's second partner is a lawyer of wide reputation, the highly esteemed Stephen T. Logan. David Davis, who will become an associate justice of the US Supreme Court, calls Logan "the best natural lawyer" of his time.

Logan teaches Lincoln to be disciplined and well prepared, and he gives Lincoln a life lesson that Lincoln never forgets: *Spend more time thinking about what your opponent is going to say than what you're going to say.* Taking that lesson to heart, Lincoln will say that he never afterwards is surprised by the strength of an opponent's argument, but is sometimes surprised by its weakness.

It is not too long before Lincoln has his own firm, Lincoln & Herndon. The Herndon of the firm is William Henry Herndon, a studious, college-educated, hard-drinking, abolitionist who is nine years younger than Lincoln. Thus begins a remarkable lifelong friendship that is never poisoned by an angry word.

The practice is interrupted only by Lincoln's two years in Congress. Lincoln returns, and business goes on as usual. Years later, when Lincoln departs for the White House, he tells "Billy" to leave the Lincoln & Herndon sign hanging where it is.

Lincoln will try more than 5,000 cases. In all, Lincoln has twenty-three years of experience at the bar, beginning in 1837, when he is twenty-eight years old.

Obama

Obama does not ride the judicial circuit, or form his own law firm, as Lincoln did. But Obama does make a mark in the field of law. He receives his law degree from one of the most prestigious educational institutions in the world, Harvard Law School. Here he learns to think like a lawyer, amidst some of the brightest and best in the legal field. In a student body that is legendary for its competitiveness, Obama achieves one of the school's most glittering prizes. He is chosen editor of its *Law Review.*

After receiving his law degree from Harvard Law School, Obama is head-hunted by the Chicago law firm of Davis, Miner, Barnhill & Galland—today known as Miner, Barnhill & Galland. The firm, founded in 1971, specializes in civil rights litigation and economic development. He helps to represent clients in civil and voting rights matters, as well as wrongful firings. Obama argues a case before a federal appellate court, and takes the lead in writing a suit to expand voter registration.

In a *Chicago Sun-Times* interview, Obama says, "I was an associate, and a lot of my work was in research and writing. I was one of the better writers. I ended up doing the more cerebral writing, less trial work." After three years as a full-time associate, he is elected to the State Senate, and becomes listed as "of counsel," until he is elected to the US Senate.
Obama's law license is currently inactive, which has given rise to an urban legend.

A few facts are in order. The Attorney Registration & Disciplinary Commission of Illinois lists President Obama's registration status as "Voluntarily retired." It lists Michelle Obama's status as "Voluntarily inactive." Attorneys with active licenses must pay annual dues, and meet continuing education requirements—in Illinois, thirty hours every two years. A senator or a president, even if he could afford the annual dues, might find it difficult to take the required continuing education courses.

Urbanlegends.about.com carries this analysis: "It's not true that either of them surrendered his or her law license to avoid disciplinary action or criminal prosecution. Nor is it true, contrary to what has been claimed on literally thousands of anti-Obama blogs and websites, that the Obamas were 'disbarred' or had their law licenses 'revoked.' Neither the Illinois State Bar Association nor the ARDC lists any accusations of misconduct or disciplinary actions against the Obamas. Quite to the contrary, a notice on the website of the Illinois State Bar says that the Association is 'proud' to have Barack and Michelle Obama as honorary members."

In *Dreams from My Father,* Obama comments on what the law is: "The law is…a memory; the law also records a long-running conversation, a nation arguing with its conscience."

Both Have Early Defeats

Lincoln is defeated the first time he runs for the Illinois legislature.

Obama is defeated the first time he runs for Congress.

Both Serve in the Illinois Legislature

Neither is born in Illinois, but both choose the state, and the state adopts them.

Lincoln serves eight years in the Illinois legislature from 1834 through 1842—four two-year terms.

Obama serves seven years from 1997 to 2004.

Both Serve in Congress

Lincoln serves one term—two years—in the House.

Obama serves three years in the Senate.

Both Are Ardent Supporters of Infrastructure Financing

Lincoln

Lincoln begins his political career as a Whig. He supports "internal improvements." When he is twenty-seven, Lincoln publishes a list of his beliefs. It states: "I go for distributing the proceeds of the sales of the public lands to the several states, to enable our state, in common with others, to dig canals and construct railroads." Many years later, when he is president, the transcontinental railroad is begun.

Obama

Obama includes major funding for infrastructure in his stimulus package; He campaigns for additional infrastructure funds in 2011—50 billion dollars—but can't get Congress to pass it.

Public Opinion Turns against Their Predecessors

Lincoln and Obama

Challenges overtake both James Buchanan and George W. Bush.

In 1860, South Carolina lets it be known that it is planning to secede from the Union. General Winfield Scott sends Buchanan a letter recommending that he reinforce the federal forts in the South. To General Scott, this kind of talk sounds like the 1830s all over again. The old general gave the same advice to President Andrew Jackson. Andrew Jackson sent Scott to Charleston to make sure the recommendation was carried out.

But James Buchanan is no Andrew Jackson. Buchanan equivocates; he tries to negotiate with states' righters. Meanwhile the forts and armories are seized by rebels. He tries to please everybody, but, as the old saying predicts, he ends up pleasing nobody. Buchanan will not use force because he believes using force is unconstitutional. He also believes that the states do not have a constitutional right to secede. His good intentions do not save him. He ends up failing totally. He leaves the White House a beaten man.

Buchanan's reputation has never recovered. Some historians say he is the worst American president ever.

Both Buchanan and Bush are limited by their beliefs and ideology. Buchanan believes that using military force to stop secession is unconstitutional. Bush is so committed to free market ideology that he is reluctant to intervene in the economic crisis. He wants to believe that the marketplace will correct itself. That's what he's been taught.

Free-market people are unfazed by the carnage, unconvinced the threat is real. They ascribe God-like attributes to the market. It is omniscient, all-seeing. If left alone, the market will determine the correct price of everything. But it must be left alone. It's like a sacred ark. Touch it, and you die.

On Bush's watch, the largest bankruptcy in American history— Lehman Brothers—occurs. The housing bubble bursts. Credit markets close down.

When he finally does intervene, Bush's leadership is weak, ineffective.

His Secretary of Treasury Henry Paulson, Jr. finally convinces Bush to act, but Bush is unable to get support from his own party. When Paulson's bailout plan is put to a vote in the House of Representatives on Monday, September 29, not a single Republican votes yes. The Dow falls 18 percent in one week— the biggest weekly drop in the history of the Dow.

Gone are the days when Bush is immensely popular. His support has fallen steadily as the Iraq War has dragged on. And now this.

When George W. Bush leaves office, he's under attack by Democrats, and disowned by Republicans. His approval numbers are abysmally low. In 2012 Bush tells Politico how he feels about national politics: "I crawled out of the swamp, and I'm not crawling back in."

Both Are Obscure Candidates

Neither is known very well until his campaign for president. If anything, Lincoln is better known in his day than Obama, but neither are big names when their campaigning begins.

Lincoln

In 1858, Lincoln is requested to write an autobiography for the campaign. And here is what Lincoln writes:

> *Born, February 12, 1809, in Hardin County, Kentucky. Education defective. Profession, a lawyer. Have been a captain of volunteers in Black Hawk war. Postmaster at a very small office. Four times a member of the Illinois legislature, and was a member of the lower house of Congress.*

Obama

Nancy Gibbs, in a special *Time* publication entitled *President Obama: The Path to the White House*, describes Obama as "a man who had been born to an idealistic white teenage mother and the charismatic African grad student who abandoned them—a man who grew up without money, talked his way into good schools, worked his way up through the pitiless world of Chicago politics to the US Senate and now the White House in a stunningly short time." Gibbs comments further: Obama's achievement, "compared with those of the Bushes or the Kennedys or the Adamses, or any of the other American princes who were born into power or bred into it, represents such a radical departure from the norm that it finally brings meaning to the promise taught from Kindergarten: 'Anyone can grow up to be President.'"

Again, a parallel. Horace Greeley, writes of Lincoln: "He was not born king of men, but (was) a child of the common people."

Lincoln and Obama Gain
National Recognition with Big Speeches

The folk philosopher Eric Hoffer tells me that talent is not uncommon. It is just uncommon to recognize it.

There is a moment when Lincoln and Obama are recognized. A moment when discerning individuals will look back and recall that this was the time when they knew they were witnessing someone who belongs on a bigger stage. In both cases, the man is asked to give a speech. The speech is really an audition for an important part in the national drama, created by decision-makers looking for an extraordinary talent. Both men do well in the audition.

Lincoln

Lincoln's breakthrough speech occurs on a snowy night in New York City on February 27, 1860. A crowd of 1,500 is packed in what was then called the Cooper Institute to see and hear the curiosity from the Wild West—the politician who almost beat US Senator Stephen Douglas in 1858.

They are in the hall tonight because this is not the kind of politician you can see just any day. There are plenty of journalists up front, pencils at the ready.

Lincoln is nervous. So are his friends. He and they are afraid he will make a fool of himself in front of sophisticated, hard-to-

19

impress, tough New Yorkers. He worries that they won't appreciate his plain, folksy, story-telling, hard-hitting speaking style. They're accustomed to elegant, flowery presentations.

He has spent hours alone, shut up in his hotel room. He has told the sponsors of the event, "I am not going to make a failure at the Cooper Institute tomorrow night if I can possibly help it."

Lincoln is introduced by William Cullen Bryant, the poet-editor at the *New-York Evening Post.* Bryant is author of the famous poem "Thanatopsis."

Lincoln says it is worth the trip just to meet Bryant. There's no false flattery here. Lincoln loves poetry, particularly morbid poems that dwell on death. He has written poems himself on the theme of "Thanatopsis"—a poem that is sometimes given the title, "A Meditation upon Death."

Lincoln begins stiffly, self-consciously, but the speech starts to build. It will end in a crescendo of oratorical power.

Lincoln has spent many hours of long, careful research. He tells the audience that virtually none of the founding fathers wanted slavery in the western territories. Lincoln can cite names and numbers. He tells how these men voted. He tells what they said in debates. He quotes from the "Northwest Ordinance of 1787," which he first read back in Indiana.

He lambastes the Dred Scott decision, deplores what it has caused.

He chides Southerners for their "my-way-or-the-highway" attitude. Lincoln's laconic wit shows through. "You will not abide the election of a Republican president! In that supposed event, you will destroy the Union, and then, you say, (that) the great crime of having destroyed it will be upon us. That is cool. A highwayman holds a pistol to my ear, and mutters through his teeth, 'stand and deliver, or I will kill you, and then you will be a murderer.'"

Lincoln urges Republicans not to be rash: "It is exceedingly desirable that all parts of this great Confederacy shall be at peace, and in harmony with one another."

Lincoln moves into his conclusion, what orators call the peroration:

> Neither let us be slandered from our duty by false accusations against us, nor frightened from it by menaces of destruction to the Government, nor of dungeons to ourselves. Let us have faith that right makes might, and in that faith, let us to the end dare to do our duty as we understand it.

The hall erupts in thunderous applause. People are yelling, screaming. A man shouts out, "He's the greatest man since St. Paul!"

The next day, four New York papers print the speech in its entirety—all one-and-a-half hours of it. Richard C. McCormick of the *New-York Evening Post* says that he "never saw an audience more thoroughly carried away by an orator."

A lawyer by the name of Charles Caverno recalls the reaction to Lincoln's speech: "The Cooper Institute speech was the turning point in the fortunes of Mr. Lincoln. Have you ever watched the turning of the tide—the slow resistless motion in one direction, and a moment later a slow resistless motion in another? That was what you could see in the East as the result of that speech. Men said as they read it, 'Well, what? Who is this?' 'Here is a strong man—a man of grasp and force. Why this man could do for the presidency.' The tide turned—set in that direction, and the result is history."

That same man, Charles Caverno, remembers when Lincoln was not a big enough name to draw a crowd, and it was not all that long before his big speech in New York City.

A few months earlier, in 1859, Lincoln is invited to give a speech at the agricultural fair in Milwaukee. There's very little interest. Caverno writes, "To Democrats, Lincoln was a beaten, discarded Illinois politician. To Republicans, Mr. Seward was the only possible candidate for the presidency."

Lincoln is supposed to give a speech from the balcony of his hotel that evening. A band is hired to draw a crowd. When eight o'clock arrives, Lincoln follows his host to look at the crowd that has assembled. But there is no crowd. No one is there except the band.

Caverno recalls what happens. Lincoln says, "Well, we can't call that a crowd, can we?" Caverno looks closely at Lincoln, and can never forget what he sees. "His countenance was fallen," he remembers. "That afterward well-known, indescribable, pathetic look of suffering sadness had taken the place of that equally indescribable smile. It was an awesome sight. He looked to me as though his soul was dreaming on something a thousand miles from that place."

His hosts think of an alternate plan, and ask Lincoln if he will give a speech inside the hotel. Lincoln agrees, and he speaks to a few people in the lobby. Early the next morning, without any notice whatsoever, Lincoln boards a train and returns to Springfield.

Obama

There is a parallel between Lincoln's humiliating experience in Milwaukee, and Obama's experience in Illinois in 2000. That year, Obama is not a big enough name to get credentials to attend the Democratic National Convention with the Illinois delegation.

But then comes 2004. Obama is asked to give a major address at the Democratic National Convention. Mary Beth Cahill, the campaign manager for John Kerry, makes the recommendation after she watches Obama steal the show at a Kerry event that spring. The decision and the speech are carefully plotted.

Obama's speech is not the equivalent of the Cooper Union address. Certainly not in length. Obama speaks for only seventeen minutes. The Cooper Union address is about ninety minutes long. Lincoln's presentation is the only speech of the evening. At the 2004 Democratic convention, John Kerry, the nominee, is the focus. But the impact of both speeches is the same. They make Lincoln and Obama national figures.

Obama works diligently. He writes out the first draft in longhand, working on it for two weeks, often many nights beyond midnight. He inserts lines he has tested on Illinois audiences, wants to make the tone personal. He sends the first draft to a Democratic speechwriting team. It is much too long, and is shortened; he is unhappy when one of his best lines is cut by Kerry's speechwriters. Obama acknowledges that his own people and Kerry's staffs edited the speech for length. But, he says, he is proud to have written the speech himself.

On *Good Morning America* the day of the speech, Obama is asked how he will deal with the fact that he opposed the invasion of Iraq, while John Kerry and John Edwards supported the resolution approving the use of military force. Obama responds that they are all focused on the future instead of looking back at the past, and that now everyone is interested in seeing a successful policy on the war. Obama also tells what Michelle told him about his big moment: "Don't screw it up."

Obama does another interview that morning, this one with NPR. Regarding the convention hall, Obama says, "I was here last night, and that really takes the pressure off; you realize that nobody's listening."

Anybody who has ever attended a national convention of either party knows that there's an enormous amount of chatter going on while most of the speeches are being made.

"So, who knows what lines I could slip in there. No one would notice; as long as I'm smiling and waving, I think I'll be OK."

But the audience does listen. He is interrupted thirty-three times by applause.

In the speech, Obama talks about his history, his mother's family, his grandfather who fought under General Patton in WWII, his grandmother who worked at a bomber plant, while raising his mother. He tells them what the name Barack means. It is an African name meaning "blessed."

He talks about how blessed he is:

I stand here today, grateful for the diversity of my heritage, aware that my parents' dreams live on in my two precious daughters. I stand here knowing that my story is part of the larger American story, that I owe a debt to all of those who came before me, and that in no other country on Earth is my story even possible.

There are some other memorable lines from the speech:

There is not a Liberal America and a Conservative America—there is the United States of America. There is not a black America and a white America and Latino America and Asian America—there's the United States of America. The pundits like to slice-and-dice our country into Red States and Blue States; Red States for Republicans, Blue States for Democrats. But I've got news for them, too: We worship an awesome God in the Blue States, and we don't like federal agents poking around in our libraries in the Red States. We coach Little League in the Blue States, and, yes, we've got some gay friends in the Red States. There are patriots who opposed the war in Iraq and there are patriots who supported the war in Iraq.

Rhetorically, he asks whether the country wishes to engage in a politics of cynicism or hope:

It's the hope of slaves sitting around a fire singing freedom songs. The hope of immigrants setting out for distant shores…The hope of a skinny kid with a funny name who believes that America has a place for him, too. Hope! Hope in the face of difficulty! Hope in the face of uncertainty!

The reaction is instant, explosive. Illinois Senator Dick Durbin says, "His public image changed because of that speech." *Time* reports that David Axelrod, who is working for the Kerry campaign, gets a copy of the speech by fax. He is astonished. "I was reading it and handing each page to my wife, and my mouth was agape," he recalls, "because it was beautiful and profound. How many people in public life can write like this?"

III.
SIMILARITIES IN TALENTS AND ABILITIES

We are always more anxious to be distinguished for a talent which we do not possess, than to be praised for the fifteen which we do possess.

– Mark Twain

SIMILARITIES IN TALENTS AND ABILITIES

Athletes

Athletics is a school where life lessons are learned: courage, discipline, focus, alertness, self-management, steadiness under pressure, strategic thinking. Athletes are not just playing. They are learning, often without knowing it. The credits are transferable: success in one field can lead to success in another. That is why so many leaders in business, the military, and politics also excelled in athletics.

George Washington, Theodore Roosevelt, and Dwight Eisenhower, and Ronald Regan come to mind. Washington was a wrestler, Roosevelt was a boxer, Ronald Regan played football and was captain of his college swim team, and Eisenhower played football and golf. Eisenhower, for example, routinely shot in the low eighties, and when the former president was seventy-seven, he hit a 104-yard hole-in-one. In the case of Lincoln and Obama, athletics shapes the way they think, the way they size up an opponent, the confidence that they feel.

Lincoln

Lincoln is in his early twenties, clerking at a store in New Salem. He already has a reputation for being somebody you shouldn't mess with.

A fight occurs at the store. There are several accounts of how it started, but according to one man who claims he saw it, some rowdies from nearby Clary's Grove pick a fight with Lincoln.

This is not a good idea. Lincoln pulls himself up to all six feet four inches, walks outside, says he'll take on any one of them. They can choose which one. There are some pretty mean fighters in that bunch. Lincoln ends up fighting the leader, a man by the name of Jack Armstrong.

We don't have many reliable details about this particular fight, but most fights in those days are brutal. Opponents try to throw one another, and in the process kick and punch and gouge and bite. Some fighters let their fingernails grow. The first thing they go for is the eyes. It's more like current cage fighting than collegiate-rules wrestling.

Lincoln fights so well, he's so strong and skilful, that the rowdies are impressed. What impresses them most is how good natured he is.

Conflict sometimes leads to friendship. Child psychologists talk about children beginning a relationship by initially fighting over a toy. And that happens with Lincoln and Armstrong. They begin a warm friendship that lasts until Armstrong's death. After his death, Lincoln successfully defends Armstrong's son Duff in a sensational murder trial. Lincoln will not take a cent from Armstrong's widow for his services.

Lincoln becomes widely known as a champion wrestler. Old-timers remember that he wore a special kind of handkerchief that men who wrestled a lot wore. When he visits some of his relatives, they refer to him as a well-known wrestler. When he wrestles, men bet on him, and usually win.

Lincoln's first law partner John Todd Stuart calls the fight with Jack Armstrong a "turning point" in Lincoln's life, one of several that will occur. It affects how Lincoln feels about himself, increases his self-confidence. It affects how others feel about him. People admire athletic prowess.

Gen. James Grant Wilson remembers a conversation he had with Lincoln in the White House. Wilson mentions that George Washington was the strongest man of his day, and a famous wrestler who never was thrown.

Lincoln responds, "It's rather curious but that is exactly my record. I could out-lift any man in Southern Illinois when I was young. And I never was thrown. There was a big fellow named Jack Armstrong who was strong as a Russian bear, that I could not put down, nor could he get me on the ground. If George was loafing around here now, I should be glad to have a match with him, and I rather believe that one of the plain people of Illinois would be able to manage the aristocrat of old Virginia."

When he is in his 50s, Lincoln can still extend a heavy axe on a horizontal line. The axe head does not wobble. Lincoln visits the troops. A young soldier is using an axe to cut wood. Lincoln takes the axe from him, holds it out straight in front of him. The soldier tries to do it, and can't.

A few months later, the man who does Lincoln's autopsy marvels at the president's sinewy muscularity.

Obama

On his surprise visit to American troops, Obama stops in Kuwait. The troops gather in a makeshift auditorium that has a basketball court. Hundreds of troops are there. Millions more will watch on TV and YouTube. Obama picks up a ball, stretches, dribbles a few times, goes to the three-point line, and drills it. His first shot. The ball barely ripples the net. The troops go wild.

Obama could have really embarrassed himself. What if it had been an air ball? *Phew!*

But Obama is a good athlete, and he knows it. He played on the Punahou High School basketball team in Honolulu in the 1970s. His team won the state championship.

Every March, Obama fills out college basketball tournament brackets with Andy Katz of ESPN. It's called Barack-etology. He'll play pickup games, or "horse," with friends, with his brother-in-law Craig Robinson, who's the current head men's basketball coach at Oregon State University, or with whomever. During the 2008 primaries, he's in North Carolina, and scrimmages with the legendary Tar Heels men's basketball team. He also loves golf. Doesn't play as much as Eisenhower did, but enough to get criticism from opponents for neglecting his presidential duties.

Impressive Communicators

Words can reveal thoughts, conceal pain, paint dreams, correct errors, and pass along dearly bought lessons to the latest generation.

Words can transport knowledge from the past, interpret the present, and speak to the future. Words can build walls between people, or bridges. Words can tear down or build up, wound or heal, tarnish or cleanse.

Words can endear you to your fellows, win them to your side, and enable you to rise to heights you may now only dream of.
– Gene Griessman, *Lincoln on Communication*

The connection between leadership and communication has been recognized in every generation, political persuasion, and religious tradition. It is difficult to think of a great leader at any time in history or field of endeavor who was not an effective communicator. Pericles is credited with saying "He who cannot communicate his ideas stands at the same level as he who has no ideas." The Bible has this pithy observation, "If the trumpet give an uncertain sound, who shall prepare himself to the battle?"

Lincoln

For years Lincoln has been called the best stump speaker in the West. Even when Lincoln was a youth, people claim they could see it coming. Sometimes on Sundays, at the little Baptist church in Indiana where his parents were members, he would ask some of his friends to join him in the woods just across the road, after the service. And when they had gathered, Lincoln would repeat the preacher's sermon, word for word, story by story, gesture by gesture, shout by shout. Lincoln was already getting a reputation for his memory and his mimicry and his oratory.

And then there was the debating society in New Salem at the Rutledge tavern, and another one in Springfield at Joshua Speed's store. Lincoln would stand on his feet, and argue a point.

Lincoln learns how to give a stump speech. That's what people called political speeches in those days. Stump speeches. His first stump speeches of record are given just after he returns from the war. He loses that first race, but Lincoln gets a good many votes, enough to encourage him. Plus he is gaining experience communicating.

Lincoln becomes a lawyer, and he gets a reputation as a good extemporaneous speaker. He has to in order to survive. Lawyers who can't give a speech are soon doing something else for a living.

A legal historian writes: "The flamboyance, tricks and courtroom antics of nineteenth-century lawyers were more than a matter of personality; this behavior created reputation; and a courtroom lawyer who did not impress the public and gain a reputation would be hard-pressed to survive."

Lincoln says essentially the very same thing in his notes for a law lecture: "Extemporaneous speaking should be practiced and cultivated. It is the lawyer's avenue to the public. However able and faithful he may be in other respects, people are slow to bring him business if he cannot make a speech."

Lincoln never writes a full-fledged book, only parts of three campaign biographies. But for years he writes poetry, letters to the editor, many of them anonymous, thousands of legal documents, notes, fragments, speeches, musings. But it is not until Lincoln becomes president that he begins to gain recognition for his literary ability.

"Perhaps no point in the career of Abraham Lincoln has excited more surprise or comment," writes Lincoln's secretary John G. Nicolay, "than his remarkable power of literary expression."

When you hear a speech by a famous politician, generally you don't know who actually wrote it, the politician or a speech writer. In Lincoln's case, the writer is Lincoln. He may include a sentence or a paragraph that someone has suggested or drafted, but Lincoln is the principal craftsman.

Noah Brooks, a journalist and editor, has an opportunity to observe Lincoln compose important messages. He leaves a snapshot of the president working on a speech, in this case, the President's Message to Congress: "It is a favorite habit of the president, when writing anything requiring thought, to have a number of slips of board or boxboard near at hand, and seated at ease in his armchair, he lays the slip on his knee, and writes and rewrites in pencil what is afterward copied in his own hand, with new changes and interlineations...Then being set up by the printer, spaces half an inch are left between each line in the proof ...more corrections and interlineations are made, and from this patchwork, the document is finally set up and printed."

Lincoln double-checks and triple-checks, and edits and re-edits. He writes between the lines. He makes sure the words are right before the public sees or hears them. If you get a chance to look at an original draft of a Lincoln speech or important document, you see words crossed out, with new phrases, sentences and paragraphs added. Lincoln is not a first-draft speaker or writer.

The Inaugural Address is a special production. He has several copies printed so that he can share what he plans to say with readers whose opinion he trusts. He tries out parts of his top-secret, highly sensitive speech on a few of them.

Lincoln asks William Seward to take a look. He recommends a closing paragraph. That paragraph will become one of the greatest paragraphs ever written. Seward proposes a draft of his own. It has long, rambling, run-together sentences.

Lincoln sees something in it, though. He asks Seward to try again. The new version is shorter, but still clumsy. Lincoln takes it in hand.

In the final version, there is a beautiful expression—*"the better angels of our nature."* How these words find their way into the First Inaugural Address is a little tale of its own.

Seward's rough draft, which has been preserved, contains the expression "better angel." Charles Dickens had used "better angels" in several of his novels. So had Shakespeare in Sonnet 144 and *Othello.*

When Lincoln reads Seward's rough draft, he notices that Seward has scratched out the words "better angel" and substituted "guardian angel of the nation."

Lincoln likes the words "better angel," and puts those words back in the speech. Seward's discarded two words from Dickens and

Shakespeare thus become the memorable expression *"the better angels of our nature."*

The speech writing comes to an end, and the big day for giving his first inaugural speech is dawning. It is around five in the morning, Monday, March 4, 1861.

A crowd is gathering down at the Capitol. Bands are tuning up. Cavalry horses are clip-clopping down Pennsylvania Blvd. Troops are filing into place. Sharpshooters are nesting in strategic spots, ready just in case there's trouble. There could be trouble. Death threats have picked up in recent days.

Lincoln is pensive, not as much about assassins as about his speech, knowing this could be his last chance to speak directly to Southern lawmakers. Some have already left Washington for home, for good.

Lincoln usually reads what he writes out loud to himself, but for this speech he wants somebody else to read it to him. He asks his son Bob to do it.

The speech is a good one, a great one really. In it, Lincoln predicts that the Union will survive: "Though passion may have strained, it must not break our bonds of affection. The mystic chords of memory, stretching from every battle-field, and patriot grave, to every living heart and hearthstone, all over this broad land, will yet swell the chorus of the Union, when again touched, as surely they will be, by the better angels of our nature."

When you hear the word *communicate* or *communicator*, you think of someone saying something to you. But great communicators understand how important it is for them to be able to listen.

Presidents can get trapped in the White House, held captive by their advisors, hearing just what the advisors want them to hear. Lincoln understands this, and does something about it. In Washington, he opens the White House to the people just like Andrew Jackson did. He sets aside certain times of the week to meet ordinary people. They will stand in line for hours to petition for a job, complain, ask for favors, tell him how they feel about what's going on, or just shake his hand. He will greet a mechanic or clerk, business owner or carpenter or soldier's mother just as graciously as he will a governor.

"What do these people know," a military officer asks. He tells Lincoln all this is a waste of time.

Lincoln responds, "No hours of my day are better employed...Men moving only in an official circle are apt to become merely official...(and) forget that they only hold power in a representative capacity. Now this is all wrong. I go into these promiscuous receptions of all who claim to have business with me twice each week, and every applicant for audience has to take his turn as if waiting to be shaved in a barber shop...I call these receptions my 'public opinion baths...'"

Obama

President Obama is a superb communicator. No doubt about it. He, like Lincoln, knows how to combine logic and emotion. He, like Lincoln, is a powerful persuader. He, like Lincoln, knows how to use the media to enlarge his audience.

A professional speaker is telling some acquaintances that there's not a speaker alive today who is Obama's equal when it comes to giving a speech before tens of thousands. He says nobody today even comes close. No politician, no TV preacher, no professional speaker. There are few who have been his equal in recent memory: Billy Graham in his prime, and JFK, and MLK, Ronald

Reagan and Bill Clinton. That's the company Obama is in. In front of tens of thousands—that's how many were at Denver—Obama today is in a league of his own. I don't know how he does it. All this talk about a teleprompter! Show me anybody who can hold an audience as big as that Denver crowd, with or without a prompter.

Obama's chief speechwriter Jon Favreau likens what he does to being the batting coach for Ted Williams. That's high praise. Every baseball fan knows you don't get any better than Ted Williams. According to the *Washington Post,* Favreau (or "Favs," as Obama calls him) is more of a speech arranger than a speech writer. Typically, Favreau will sit with Obama for thirty minutes or so, and write down everything the president says. Then, Favreau writes what he heard, gets edits from Obama, and does another draft.

"He could read the telephone directory and it would sound good," says Ted Widmer, editor of an acclaimed edition of American political speeches, and a former Bill Clinton speechwriter.

Obama, just like Lincoln, combines writing and speaking skills. Both of them prepare diligently. There's no winging it on a big speech. He gets ready like Lincoln—reading books, looking at other people's speeches, shutting himself up to think, to write.

Soon after the 2008 campaign kicks off, Obama is scheduled to speak in the all-important state of Iowa for the Jefferson-Jackson fundraiser. Hillary Clinton will also speak at the same event. Obama spends hours in hotel rooms, day after day, memorizing and rehearsing. He road-tests some of the lines at a campaign stop in Spartanburg, South Carolina. When the night finally comes, Obama knocks the ball out of the park. The ovation when Obama finishes is deafening.

Obama has been writing for a long time. He writes *Dreams from My Father* nine years before his campaign for the US Senate. It is lyrical, poignant, superbly written. *Time* magazine's Joe Klein says *Dreams from My Father* may be "the best written memoir ever produced by an American politician."

Obama reportedly received a six-figure advance to write that book. It was originally supposed to be a book about race relations. As the book developed, the story became more personal, more about Obama's own journey.

He struggles to finish it. Obama has kept a journal, and like Lincoln, he has written poems, but he has never done a book before. His half-sister says that Obama eventually retreated for several months with his wife, Michelle, "to find a peaceful sanctuary where there were no phones."

Like Lincoln, Obama loves poetry. It shapes his thinking, his writing, his speaking. T.S. Eliot is one of his favorite poets. He especially likes the poem "East Coker" from *Four Quartets.*

Obama writes a letter to his girlfriend at Columbia when he is in his early twenties. He recommends *Four Quartets,* and mentions Eliot's fatalism, which he says he feels himself. Again, shades of Lincoln and his fatalism.

The poem has the feel of a speech Lincoln gives in Springfield when he is twenty-nine years old. Lincoln asks: "Is it unreasonable to expect that some man possessed of the loftiest genius, coupled with ambition sufficient to push it to its utmost stretch, will at some time, spring up among us?"

At press conferences, Obama does not sound very poetic, or all that articulate. He sounds more like a college professor responding to a question in a graduate seminar. He doesn't do set pieces in press conferences the way Newt Gingrich does.

Maybe it's because Obama has learned what Lincoln learned, that every single word of a president will be parsed and analyzed, criticized or applauded. Lincoln was really good at extemporary speaking, but he gave it up after he became president—for the same reason. Lincoln put it this way: "I determined to be so clear that no honest man could misunderstand me, and no dishonest man could successfully misrepresent me."

In Lincoln's day, the media consisted mainly of newspapers, pamphlets, tracts, booklets and books. Today there's all that, plus TV and talk radio, blogs and emails, streaming video and digital radio.

When you are president in the twenty-first century, the press follows you everywhere. And if the press doesn't catch your oops moment, somebody with a smart phone will, and it will be on YouTube within minutes, and looped incessantly on TV and radio and streaming video and talked about on the blogs. If you're president and you misspeak, it can trigger a sell-off on Wall Street.

So Obama chooses every word carefully, rephrases, takes long pauses. Sounds un-poetic, but that's the reason. Obama, like Lincoln, wants to make it difficult for the dishonest to successfully misrepresent him. But they will try anyway.

There are reports that White House advisors had debates about which is more important, messaging or governing during the fights over the health care bill (Affordable Care Act, or ACA) and the stimulus bill. Obama recognized that if the health care bill or the stimulus bill could be broken into smaller parts, and voted on part by part, the plans would be easier to explain, easier to sell.

But Obama is told that they do not have enough time to do that. And the economy is too fragile. He may not get the votes he needs if he waits. So messaging is given a secondary role. And a price is paid. To this day, millions of Americans don't know that there are features in the ACA that they strongly support, but they're negative about the bill as a whole.

Same thing with the Recovery Act—the stimulus bill. The public strongly supports lots of its components, like infrastructure and assistance to states for teachers and firefighters, but the public has been convinced that the stimulus itself is a failure. They think Obama has raised taxes. He hasn't. In fact, the stimulus contains one of the largest tax rebates in American history. But the public doesn't know it.

Obama acknowledges that he should have done a better job at messaging during the early months. Maybe he couldn't have. Maybe his advisors were right.

But by the fourth year of his presidency, Obama has taken to heart Lincoln's belief that public sentiment is everything. With it, everything is possible. Without it, nothing is possible. He has learned that messaging is governing.

Governing is listening. Obama, like Lincoln at his "public opinion baths" seems to feel at home when he is listening. Rudyard Kipling's words come to mind: "If you can talk with crowds and keep your virtue, Or walk with Kings—nor lose the common touch."

You sense that Obama truly enjoys the role of observer. You see him watching, listening, making note of things in *Dreams from My Father*. That quality is essential when you are a community organizer—a job famously mocked by Republican vice-presidential nominee Sarah Palin. "I guess a small-town mayor is sort of like a community organizer, except that you have actual responsibilities."

There is one responsibility that community organizers have: listening. How can you organize a community without listening to its people? How else will you know what the common denominators are? How else will you know what people want, and what they are most likely to respond to? Max Ehrmann's words could have been written for community organizers, or presidents: "Speak your truth quietly and clearly, and listen to others, even the dull and ignorant; they too have their story."

Listening is more than an act. It is an attitude—an attitude based on the belief that one can learn from others, whether high or low.

INSPIRING LEADERS

Lincoln and Obama are leaders, and they know it. Lincoln is such a great leader that he's still studied in literally thousands of leadership seminars. The best-seller *Lincoln on Leadership* by Donald T. Phillips is often used as a text. Obama has the same extraordinary capacity to evoke love and inspire sacrificial efforts from supporters.

The leadership style of Lincoln and Obama is not rigid, dictatorial, or dogmatic. By temperament and inclination, Lincoln and Obama value discussion, and encourage it. They are anything but dogmatic.

The career path that Lincoln and Obama follow rarely rewards authoritative leadership styles. Lawyers and community organizers do not generally have the authority to order people around. Maybe their assistants and staff, but usually not their clients, and certainly not judges and juries. Lawyers and community organizers get their power from persuading, from convincing.

By contrast, generals do give commands. A general can give an order, and if you disobey, you can be jailed, and in some instances shot.

There are exceptions. General Dwight Eisenhower, for example, gave commands and issued orders. But in his capacity as Supreme Commander Allied Expeditionary Force for the Battle of Normandy, Eisenhower needed to convince a fractious team of leaders to execute Operation Overlord. That experience prepared Eisenhower for the presidency, where power comes from persuading and convincing.

Lincoln

Horace Greeley writes that Lincoln "made himself a great persuader, therefore a leader, by dint of firm resolve, patient effort, and dogged perseverance..." Look through all the interviews that Billy Herndon conducted with people who knew Lincoln, and you will not find anyone calling Lincoln autocratic or dictatorial.

In fact, when Lincoln becomes president, his Secretary of War Edwin Stanton thinks Lincoln is too indecisive, too wishy-washy for leadership in a crisis. Stanton tells an acquaintance that he, Stanton, will have to make a president out of Lincoln.

Whether on his own, or because Stanton and others prodded him, Lincoln does become more decisive, more authoritative.

Lincoln gets more power than any other president in history. But even with his immense power—there are over a million men in uniform by war's end—Lincoln is always talking to people, consulting, getting their input before making a final decision.

Obama

Obama grows up caught between two worlds, one black, the other white. He refers to family gatherings as a "little mini-United Nations:" Obama learns to be a harmonizer. Lincoln recognized the same impulse in himself, thinks of himself as a harmonizer as he tries to work with moderates, conservatives, and radical Republicans.

A classmate of Obama's at Harvard Law School remembers that Obama was elected president of the *Law Review,* the first African-American ever to hold that position, because of Obama's ability to win over the conservatives. "Most of the class were liberals, but there was a growing conservative Federalist Society presence, and there were real fights between right and left about almost every issue. Barrack won the election because the conservatives thought he would take their arguments into account."

Obama meets Betsy Myers, who will be his future chief operating officer of the 2008 political campaign. He tells her there will be three ruling principles in his operation: One. Run the campaign with respect. Two. Build it from the bottom up. Three. No drama.

Obama says he wants to run the campaign like a business, and in a good business the customer is king.

Obama tells a reporter, "As somebody who has been a community organizer, I was convinced that if you invited people to get engaged, if you weren't trying to campaign like you were selling soap, but instead said, 'This is your campaign. You own it, and you can run with it' that people would respond, and we could build a new electoral map."

He runs his 2008 campaigner as a harmonizer, as someone who brings people together.

IV.
SIMILARITIES IN TEMPERAMENT

Temperament lies behind mood; behind will lies the fate of character. Then behind both, the influence of family, the tyranny of culture; and finally the power of climate and environment; and we are free, only to the extent we rise above these.

– John Burroughs

SIMILARITIES IN TEMPERAMENT

Both Are Resolute

Resolve, like the other traits in this section, is not unique to either Lincoln or Obama. Take any of America's notable presidents—George Washington, Andrew Jackson, Theodore Roosevelt, Franklin Delano Roosevelt, Harry Truman, Dwight Eisenhower—all are remarkably resolute.

> Resolve is present so often in successful careers that it can be thought of as essential to high achievement in any area, not just politics.

Lincoln

A young man writes to Lincoln asking for advice. He's thinking about becoming a lawyer. Lincoln replies, "If you are resolutely determined to make a lawyer of yourself, the thing is more than half gone already." On another occasion Lincoln writes, "Always bear in mind that your own resolution to succeed is more important than any other one thing."

One day a letter arrives at the White House. It's from Lincoln's son Robert. The young man tells his father about a friend of his, a classmate who is flunking out of school. The friend is despondent, and has almost given up.

Lincoln finds time to pull away from the incessant demands of a nation at war to write a letter to the struggling student. And this is what Lincoln says: "'Must' is the word. I know not how to aid you, save in the assurance of one of mature age, and much severe experience, that you cannot fail, if you resolutely determine, that you will not."

Obama

Obama is making a speech in 2006, four full years before he will become president. He tells a journalist, "Making your mark on the world is hard. If it were easy, everybody would do it. But it's not. It takes patience, it takes commitment, and it comes with plenty of failure along the way. The real test is not whether you avoid this failure, because you won't. It's whether you let it harden or shame you into inaction, or whether you learn from it; whether you choose to persevere."

You cannot read accounts of Obama's uphill battles during the primary without feeling his resolve, sensing his persistence.

Once in office, Obama will not give up on things he believes in. He persists in trying to change Washington, as he puts it, long after it is clear to many observers that he will not be able to bring Democrats and Republicans together.

That does not happen, but what does happen is a string of legislative victories during his first two years that equal any previous administration, and more than most. The victories dismay his opponents. At a press conference, Obama says, "I am persistent. I am persistent. You know, if I believe in something strongly, I stay on it."

Both Are Good-Natured

Lincoln

Amiability is not a pose for Lincoln. It comes out of his soul. A visitor observes that while Lincoln sits and talks politics, his little boys "clambered over his long legs, patted his cheeks, pulled his nose, and poked their fingers in his eyes, without causing reprimand or even notice."

Lincoln is known for his good-natured disposition, his hearty laugh. Time and again during the days after his election, visitors from the South make trips to Springfield to observe first-hand the Republican ogre. They expect to find a vile, hateful, despicable monster. Instead they meet a friendly, folksy, good-natured man who invites them into his office, tells them a joke or two. They leave Lincoln's office still convinced that slavery is worth fighting for, and killing Yankees is not all that bad, but willing to admit that Lincoln himself seems like a good person.

Obama

He is known for his smile, his pleasant disposition, his willingness to reach out to people. Early in his administration, there's an ugly episode involving a black Harvard University professor by the name of Henry Louis Gates and a white Cambridge, Massachusetts policeman named James Crowley. The professor is arrested. Angry words are exchanged. The incident makes international news, threatens to raise racial tensions.

The president plays the role of peacemaker, invites both of them to the White House. They accept, and join the President Obama and Vice President Joe Biden in the Rose Garden for a beer. The meeting becomes known as "the beer summit." It's so cordial, the professor and the policeman plan to meet again. Obama says afterward he's convinced "what brings us together is stronger than what pulls us apart." Gates and Cowley issue statements praising the president.

Both Love to Hear Jokes, Love to Tell Them

Humor can cool tempers, heal wounds, win over an opponent, disarm a foe, and laugh a bad idea out of existence. Humor can be a terrible swift sword in the hands of a great leader.

> One good way to destroy an opponent is to turn him into a joke.

Lincoln

There is a wry wit about Lincoln. In his campaign autobiography, he says, "If any personal description of me is thought desirable, it may be said, I am, in height, six feet, four inches, nearly; lean in flesh, weighing on an average one hundred and eighty pounds; dark complexion, with coarse black hair, and grey eyes—no other marks or brands recollected." Marks or brands recollected! A little joke.

One of Lincoln's old friends remembers a joke that he told about the Revolutionary War hero Ethan Allen. It is earthy, like many of Lincoln's stories. In this story, Ethan Allen visits England after the war, and discovers there's a picture of George Washington in a privy. His English host wants to know what Allen thinks about it. Ethan Allen says he thinks it is very appropriate. Says if there's anything that will make an Englishman shit fast, it's George Washington.

Another friend says Lincoln could make a cat laugh. He remembers a Lincoln story. It's about a bashful young man who becomes a married man with five little bashful boys. He and his red-headed wife become Millerites. Now the Millerites believed that the world would come to an end on March 21, 1843.

Before they ascend in the Rapture, the two of 'em agree to make a clean breast of it to each other.

The man insists that his wife should go first, as she has promised in her marriage vow to obey her husband.

"Well dear," says she, "our little Sammy is not your child."
"Well," says the husband, "whose is he?"

"Oh dear," says she, "he is the one-eyed shoemaker's. He came to see me once when you was away, and in a vile hour, I gave way."

"Well," says the husband, "is the rest mine?"

"No," says she.

"And whose are they?" says he.

"Oh, dear," says she, "they belong ... to the neighborhood."

"Well," says the man, "I'm ready to leave. Gabriel, blow your horn!"

Lincoln knows himself, knows who he is. He tells a group of friends, "It was a common notion that those who laughed heartily often never amounted to much—never made great men." He paused, and added, "If this be the case, farewell to all my glory."

The journalist Henry Villard writes this about Lincoln: "I think it would be hard to find one who tells better jokes, enjoys them better, and laughs oftener than Abraham Lincoln."

Villard spends several months with Lincoln in Springfield, Illinois from the time he was elected until he is sworn in as president. Villard's careful observations are one of our very best sources of insider information about this time in Lincoln's life.

Here are several statements Villard wrote: "His never-failing stories helped many times to heal wounded feelings and mitigate disappointments...None of his hearers enjoyed the wit—and wit was an unfailing ingredient of his stories—half as much as he did himself...It was a joy indeed to see the effect on him. A high-pitched laughter lighted up his otherwise melancholy countenance with thorough merriment. His body shook all over with gleeful emotion..."

Lincoln's humor, like that of many humorists today, often does not translate well to the printed page. That is because Lincoln relied on voice inflections, contortions of his face, timing, pauses, the use of various dialects, and the setting itself to make a story funny. It was not just the story that worked. It was how and when Lincoln told it.

As an example, here is one story that Lincoln told Thurlow Weed, a powerful political operator from New York. Weed, who traveled to Springfield to meet with the president-elect, said he never forgot the story. The two of them got into an extended conversation about possible cabinet choices. One name that came up was Henry Winter Davis, a Republican congressman from Maryland.

Weed's mentioning the state of Maryland prompted Lincoln to tell a joke about a very old man who appeared in court as a witness. The judge asked the man how old he was. He replied that he was sixty. The judge, who knew the man was lying, repeated the question, and received the same answer. "I happen to know you are older than sixty," the judge said, and gave him a warning about lying. The man then said, "You're probably thinking about them fifteen years I lived in Maryland, which was just so much lost time. So them years don't count."

It is well established that Lincoln had a number of quips at the ready. He was, in this respect, like seasoned comedians who work the clubs. What seems to be spontaneous is really a response that is developed well in advance.

Lincoln loves puns, word play. In a courtroom on the circuit, an opposing lawyer's suspenders give way, his pants fall, exposing his behind. Lincoln says he will refrain from making any further remarks "with the end in view." During the war he comments on an Army captain who has been caught furtively watching women undress. Lincoln recommends that the officer should be elevated to "peerage" with title of "Count Peeper."

"Mr. Lincoln has not altered one bit; he amused us nearly all evening telling funny stories and cracking jokes," a visitor to

Springfield writes. "I could hardly believe that I was sitting in the august presence of a real live president."

Jokes become Lincoln's therapy. "A funny story, if it has the element of genuine wit...puts new life into me," he says of himself. "If it were not for these stories—jokes—jests, I should die."

Long before scientific evidence demonstrates that laughter can actually prevent disease, and sometimes cure it, Lincoln speaks of laughter as medicine. He realizes that laughter can be an anesthetic that will help him bear pain. Congressman Isaac N. Arnold remembers hearing Lincoln's distinctive laughter ringing through the White House while he and a delegation wait to be admitted to the president's office. He remarks: "That laugh has been the president's life-preserver."

One very bad day, the cabinet assembles to assess the news from the front. Lincoln begins the meeting by reading a newspaper article written by one of his favorite humorous writers. Several of the cabinet members are not amused. Several of them in fact never are. One asks, "Mr. President, how can you laugh on a day like this?" Lincoln replies, "I laugh to keep from crying—that's all, that's all."

Obama

There's a playfulness in his temperament.

It's January 2012 and President Obama is at Harlem's Apollo Theater. He breaks into the opening of Al Green's recording of "Let's Stay Together." A month later, he is hosting a tribute to the blues at the White House and sings the first few lines of "Sweet Home Chicago," with encouragement from B.B. King and Buddy Guy, while Mick Jagger, another performer at the event, claps along.

Mark McKinnon, who's a Republican strategist, and a one-time Nashville songwriter, says that these kinds of things make the president more likable. "It's humanizing," he notes. McKinnon uses a baseball analogy: "Just the fact that he tried to sing in public was a single. That he sang well was a double. That he didn't sing 'America the Beautiful' was a triple. That he sang Al Green was a home run."

McKinnon's reference to "American the Beautiful" is a slap at Mitt Romney, who sings lamentable renditions of the classic.

Obama does come across as human and humorous. That's a plus. Americans aren't crazy about all Obama's programs by any means, but poll after poll show that lots of Americans like the man a lot.

It is at the roasts where Obama shines. He turns his wit on himself, on hot issues, on his good friends, and on his opponents.

On himself: "Good evening, everybody, I would like to welcome you to the ten-day anniversary of my First One Hundred Days. During the Second One Hundred Days, we will design, build and open a library dedicated to my First One Hundred Days. My next One Hundred Days will be so successful, I will complete them in seventy-two days. And on the seventy-third day, I will rest."

On Mitt Romney:
"It's great to be here this evening in the vast, magnificent Hilton ballroom—or what Mitt Romney would call a little fixer-upper."

On the Secret Service, who had just been involved in a late-night scandal in South America:
"I had a lot more material prepared, but I have to get the Secret Service home in time for their new curfew."

On Rahm Emanuel, his chief of staff, now mayor of Chicago, who is known for his take-no-prisoners approach to politics: "The truth is, when you really get to know Rahm, he does have a softer side. Very few people know that he studied ballet for a few years. In fact, he was the first to adapt Machiavelli's *The Prince* for dance. It was an intriguing piece, as you can imagine. There were a lot of kicks below the waist."

On John McCain, mocking Arizona's immigration law:
"'John McCain couldn't make it. He said he had never identified himself as a maverick. We all know what happens in Arizona when you don't have ID. Adios, amigos."

On Michele Bachmann, joking about her questioning his birthplace: "Michele Bachmann is here. I understand she is thinking about running for president, which is weird because I hear she was born in Canada. Yes, Michele, this is how it starts. Just letting you know."

On Tim Pawlenty, poking fun at his low visibility as a candidate: "Tim Pawlenty's not here, but he's hit the campaign trail hard. And to be honest, I think the American people are going to have some tough questions for Tim. Specifically, 'Who are you, and where do you come from?' Which is OK. Two years into my presidency, and I'm still getting those questions."

On "birthers":
"It's been quite a year since I've spoken here last. Lots of ups, lots of downs, except for my approval ratings, which have just gone down. But that's politics; it doesn't bother me. Besides, I happen to know that my approval ratings are still very high in the country of my birth."

On House Minority Leader John Boehner and his tan:
"We have a lot in common: He is a person of color. Although not a color that appears in the natural world."

On Sarah Palin, making reference to her response to ABC's Charles Gibson, who asked her what insights her experience gave her about the Russians (Palin had replied, "You can actually see Russia from land here in Alaska, from an island in Alaska."):"I do love the Waldorf-Astoria. You know, I hear that from the doorstep, you can see all the way to the Russian Tea Room."

On Donald Trump, mocking his nationally publicized questioning of Obama's birth certificate:
"Now, I know that he's taken some flak lately, but no one is prouder to put this birth certificate matter to rest than The Donald. And that's because he can finally get back to focusing on the issues that matter, like did we fake the moon landing? What really happened in Roswell, New Mexico?..."

Obama's one-liners sound like Lincoln telling a heckler, "You ought to know that men whose business it is to speak in public make it a part of their business to have something always ready for just such fellows as you are."

When Lincoln debates Stephen Douglas, he uses humor like a stiletto. In front of a crowd of thousands in Quincy, Illinois, Lincoln sticks it into Douglas' idea of letting citizens in the western territories vote slavery up or down, a notion that Douglas calls "popular sovereignty."

"Has it not got down as thin as the homeopathic soup that was made by boiling the shadow of a pigeon that had starved to death?"

Lincoln's thrust evokes "roars of laughter and cheering," writes a journalist at the event.

Something similar occurs during the last weeks of the 2012 presidential campaign. Obama is addressing a crowd of thousands in Fairfax, Virginia. He is describing Mitt Romney's tactic of dancing about on controversial issues:

"He's forgetting' what his own positions are, and he's betting that you will, too. He's changin' up so much. Back-stepping and side-stepping...I'm not a doctor, but we've got to name this condition that he's going through. He's forgettin' what his own positions are...I think it's called...*Romneysia.*"

The audience literally explodes with laughter and cheers when Obama names the disease, just like the audience did in Quincy, Illinois. Then Obama continues,

"If you say you'll protect a woman's right to choose, and then you stand up in a primary debate and say you'll be delighted to sign a bill outlawing that right to choose in all cases, then you've definitely got Romneysia..."

Obama grins. Chuckles.

"If you come down with a case of Romneysia, and if you can't seem to remember the policies that are still on your website, or the promises that you've made over the SIX years that you've been running for president...Here's the good news...ObamaCare covers pre-existing conditions."

Obama's riff goes viral on YouTube and the blogosphere. With good reason. It is one of the brilliant uses of humor in American political history.

Not Greedy or Acquisitive

Neither Lincoln nor Obama ever accepts the belief that greed is good. Their thinking and behavior is more aligned with the teachings of religious leaders who have counted greed among the Seven Deadly Sins. Getting as much as you can, as fast as you can, any way you can, regardless of the consequences does not appeal to either of them as a philosophy to live by.

Lincoln

Lincoln's fees are so low that a meeting is called by his fellow lawyers about the issue. They urge him to raise his fees so that they can make a decent living.

He refunds a client part of the fee that they had agreed on. Lincoln explains that he didn't do enough to earn it, even though he prevailed in the case.

Lincoln does take handsome fees from railroads, but not from the clients he calls "plain people."

A local lawyer defrauds a client, and is charged with misappropriating his client's funds. Judge David Davis chooses Lincoln as the most suitable attorney to admonish the wretch. Lincoln "skins" him. Gives him a lecture that he will never forget. Tells him that he has not only disgraced himself but harmed the profession.

Lincoln feels no need to get rich quickly.

Obama

He chooses a career path without consideration of great wealth. After serving as editor of the *Harvard Law Review,* there are plenty of career choices more financially rewarding than doing civil rights and wrongful termination litigation.

It's not that Obama is lacking in ambition. He *is* driven. He's just not driven to make vast sums of money.

Not that he's a pauper. He has made a lot of money from his books, and so has Michelle. His serious money has come from

Dreams from My Father and *The Audacity of Hope*. Just in 2007, for example, Obama reportedly earned more than $4 million from book sales.

Both Are Ambitious, Aspire to National Prominence

Lincoln

Billy Herndon describes Lincoln as "the most ambitious man in the world, a man totally swallowed up by his ambitions." This from his law partner who virtually worships the man. "Any man who thinks Lincoln calmly sat down and gathered his robes about him has a very erroneous knowledge of Lincoln," he writes. "He was always calculating, and always planning. His ambition was a little engine that knew no rest."

Obama

There can be no doubt that Obama is ambitious, and that he views ambition as a virtue. In his book *Revival,* Richard Wolffe writes, "He didn't wait his turn to run for president. Instead he leapfrogged over the party's most established, better-funded, and more connected names."

Wolffe's observation parallels something that Lincoln once said to Herndon, "You must not wait to be brought forward by the older men...Do you suppose that I should ever have got into notice if I had waited to be hunted up and pushed forward by older men?"

Obama speaks of "a poverty of ambition" in several of his speeches. It is a play on words. Poverty of ambition is a lack of ambition. It is not being willing to work hard…"We need to steer clear of this poverty of ambition, where people want to drive fancy cars and wear nice clothes and live in nice apartments but don't want to work hard to accomplish these things. Everyone should try to realize their full potential."

But "poverty of ambition" is the kind of ambition that focuses on goals that in the end will leave one impoverished in spirit. In a 2006 speech, Obama says, "Focusing your life solely on making a buck shows a poverty of ambition. It asks too little of yourself. And it will leave you *unfulfilled.*"

Lincoln and Obama Are "Cool"

Rudyard Kipling in his great poem "If" praises the ability to keep your head when all about you are losing theirs, and blaming it on you. Both Lincoln and Obama have this quality in abundance.

There are no records of Lincoln ever getting lost in revelry. No wild nights on the town. No one would think of saying to Lincoln, "Let's go out and get drunk."

When old men and women are asked to tell what comes to mind when they recall being around Lincoln, they say his calm—his steady, plodding, sad calm. The reports are so consistent they seem to bear out the observation by Aristotle that great men are always of a nature originally melancholy.

The same kind of report comes from those who are around Obama. He is calm. He is cool. They call him cool in the sense that cool means sharp, and having it together. But they also mean cool in the sense that Obama is unflappable when everybody around him is in a tizzy. Cool, as in not quickly reaching the boiling point. The same thing Horace Greeley meant when he describes Lincoln: "There was probably no year of his life when he was not a wiser, *cooler*, and better man than he had been the year preceding."

Lincoln

John Hay, another of Lincoln's private secretaries, calls him "imperturbable."

60

On his way to be inaugurated, Lincoln tells a crowd that has gathered, "Keep cool." This is Lincoln's word when tempers are boiling, gun sales are skyrocketing, and state militias are drilling. Here is the comment Lincoln makes in Pittsburgh: "My advice, then...is to *keep cool*. If the great American people will only keep their temper, on both sides of the line, the troubles will come to an end, and the question which now distracts the country will be settled."

In his younger years, Lincoln is good-natured and slow to anger, but he can be aroused. He physically "whips" more than one opponent. And he can be vicious with his pen, whether writing under his own name, a pen name or anonymously. In speeches he can demolish a foe. He ridicules a man so mercilessly in a speech that the man flees the room.

Lincoln gets so entangled in a quarrel that his opponent—James Shields, the treasurer of Illinois, challenges him to a duel. Lincoln accepts the challenge. On September 22, 1842, the two meet to settle their differences with weapons. At the last moment their seconds work out a face-saving compromise. Wayne C. Temple, the Lincoln scholar, believes this is the turning point for Lincoln.

By the time Lincoln reaches the White House, he has become the "wiser, cooler man" that Horace Greeley described. In 1863, he writes to a quick-tempered Army officer by the name of James M. Cutts: "Quarrel not at all. No man resolved to make the most of himself can spare time for personal contention. Better give your path to a dog, than be bitten by him in contesting for the right. Even killing the dog would not cure the bite."

Obama

Friends and close observers say there is an almost unshakable imperturbability about Obama as well. They speak of his "innate aversion to rush, his commitment to compromise." When they talk about him, they use expressions like "preternaturally calm, content with his own company."

He is called "No-drama Obama." He doesn't like drama. Doesn't want it around him. In most political campaigns, drama is a constant, but not Obama's. He wants his campaign to be strategic, high-energy, but no drama. He wants it run like a good business

The results of Obama's campaign philosophy show. Joe Klein, of *Time* magazine, writes: "Obama prospered throughout the 2008 campaign because of the steadiness of his temperament and the judicious quality of his decision-making. They are his best-known qualities."

Chief political advisor David Axelrod talks about "this kind of cool, centered quality. His sort of tranquility."

In fact, Obama is too calm for some of their tastes. More than one advisor says he wishes Obama would get angry more often.

One big reason Lincoln and Obama are cool is because they think and act like lawyers. Lawyers typically argue instead of quarreling. Good lawyers think strategically and avoid personal attacks. Not always, of course, because lawyering is done by humans. Tempers flare, and quarrels break out. But that is not the rule. Shakespeare, whom Lincoln memorized by the yard, writes in *The Taming of the Shrew*: "And do as adversaries do in law. Strive mightily, but eat and drink as friends."

Do It with Feeling

Lincoln and Obama are logical, methodical, and precise. David Hirsch and Dan Van Haften, in *Abraham Lincoln and the Structure of Reason*, show that Lincoln taught himself how to do a Euclidean demonstration during his days riding the judicial circuit. And he used this mathematical model as a template for his speeches and legal arguments and letters for the rest of his life. The same authors show that Obama does the same thing.

But that does not mean there are no feelings there. Still waters run deep.

Lincoln

It is February 11, 1861. Tomorrow will be his birthday. The day is cold and bleak. A somber throng of well-wishers follows the president-elect to the train station to see him off. There are old friends, and relatives, even people who didn't vote for him, but who take civic pride in their most famous citizen.

The scene becomes emotional. Many in the audience are sobbing. Lincoln, who almost always is self-contained in public, is visibly moved. An eyewitness writes, "His own breast heaved with emotion, and he could scarcely command his feelings sufficiently to commence."

Newspaper reporters who have trailed along aren't expecting much. Lincoln already told them that he's going to make just a few remarks, not give a speech.

Lincoln's words are direct, heart-felt. And they touch the crowd.

When *New York Tribune* journalist Henry Villard sees the reaction, he tells Lincoln that he thinks his words should be shared with the nation.

Lincoln agrees. And as the train pulls out of the station, Lincoln starts writing.

He begins to smooth out his words, find a cadence. What he says at the station is moving, heartfelt but rough-edged. Now all his years of reading and memorizing Shakespeare and Robert Burns and the King James Version of the Bible, and writing poetry himself, all of that begins to work for him.

His thoughts take poetic form. There are little flourishes that the experts call *antiphony:* "Here my children have been born/and one is buried." But Lincoln uses just a few of them. This is not a poetry-writing exercise.

Lincoln wants to convey a message to the nation, and the *New York Tribune* is going to help him do it. The flourishes are there to make sure he comes across as more than an uneducated rustic.

To a nation reeling from news that the Cotton States are seceding, and the Union is disintegrating, Lincoln expresses hope and confidence: "With the assistance of the Divine Being," he writes, "I cannot fail."

Lincoln virtually worships George Washington, and he would never think of himself as his equal. But Lincoln feels that the burden he is taking on is greater than the one Washington dealt with. Washington fought an external foe, the British. Lincoln knows there could be a war in which Americans will fight Americans.

Before his departure, Lincoln tries out the George Washington comparison on a friend. The words go down well, so he keeps them in the final version of his farewell remarks. Lincoln writes "...with a task before me greater than that which rested upon Washington."

Lincoln's speeches often have the cold logic of a mathematical argument. But on this day, he lets the audience briefly look into his heart, feel its beat, know his anguish.

He expresses gratitude. "To this place, and the kindness of these people"—poetry again—"I owe everything." He speaks of his family and of his little boy Eddie who is buried not far from the train station. Then he says, "I now leave, not knowing when, or whether ever, I may return…"

That sentence is raw, but he leaves it in. Lincoln has a premonition, and has spoken privately about it. He feels he will never return.

And Lincoln does not return to Springfield again, until another train returns some four and a half years later with two coffins— his own and his son Willie's—to be buried there.

Lincoln finishes his editing. Lincoln scholar Harold Holzer calls what is happening, "a stunning example not of spontaneous eloquence, but of Lincoln's meticulous ability to edit and rewrite, even under pressure." The train is speeding along now through the Illinois countryside. People are waving handkerchiefs and American flags as it passes by. The next day, this is what newspapers will say Lincoln said at the train station:

> My friends—No one, not in my situation, can appreciate my feeling of sadness at this parting. To this place, and the kindness of these people, I owe everything. Here I have lived a quarter of a century, and have passed from a young to an old man. Here my children have been born, and one is buried. I now leave, not knowing when, or whether ever, I may return, with a task before me greater than that which rested upon Washington. Without the assistance of the Divine Being who ever attended him, I cannot succeed. With that assistance I cannot fail. Trusting in Him who can go with me, and remain with you and be everywhere for good, let us confidently hope that all will yet be well. To His care commending you, as I hope in your prayers you will commend me, I bid you an affectionate farewell.

Obama

Dreams from My Father is published in 1995. It will go through many printings. Nine years later, when Obama writes the preface to the new edition, he lets us look into his heart for a moment, somewhat as Lincoln does at the train station in Springfield.

At Springfield, Lincoln says farewell to loved ones who have meant more to him than he can say. He will not see most of them ever again.

And in the preface to the new edition, Obama says farewell to his mother, whom he will never see again.

He tells us that she helped him during the final stages the book, made suggestions about how to say things, asked him to be generous to the memory of his father.

And then he lets us see his own humanness, his sadness that he did not say more about his mother, maybe that he might have written the book about her instead of about his father. This is very human, for who has not wished he could call back another time, and get to say what he did not say, do what he did not do.

It is a eulogy for his mother, kind and appreciative, sad for his loss, full of praise.

Obama writes, "She had spent the previous ten years doing what she loved. She travelled the world, working in the distant villages of Asia and Africa, helping women buy a sewing machine or a milk cow or an education that might give them a foothold in the world's economy. She gathered friends from high and low...she wrote reports, read novels, pestered her children, and dreamed of grandchildren. We saw each other frequently, our bond unbroken."

He continues, "In my daughters I see her every day, her joy, her capacity for wonder. I won't try to describe how deeply I mourn her passing still. I know that she was the kindest, most generous spirit I have ever known, and that what is best in me I owe to her."

That last sentence parallels something that Lincoln tells law partner Billy Herndon about his deceased mother, "All that I am or hope to be I owe to my angel mother."

Do the Right Thing

At business schools, MBA students work through the process of deciding whether to acquire a new company or not, whether to keep a vendor or get a new one, whether to fire an underperforming manager. The numbers are churned, the plusses and minuses are calculated, and a decision is reached. It is an old science. Benjamin Franklin described his version of assigning weights to the plusses and minuses as "prudential algebra."

But there is one question that should weigh more heavily than any other: What is the *right* thing to do? There is abundant evidence that Lincoln and Obama ask it when they make decisions.

Lincoln

One day a young man walks up the stairs to Lincoln's office. He wants to know if Lincoln & Herndon will take his case. Lincoln asks a few questions, and learns that he wants to bring suit for $600 against a widow, with six children. Six hundred dollars may not seem like much now, but it was a considerable amount then. A circuit judge made $750 a year.

After hearing the man out, Lincoln replies, "Yes, we can doubtless gain your case for you...We can distress a widowed mother and her six fatherless children, and thereby get for you six hundred dollars to which you seem to have a legal claim...But you must remember that some things legally right are not morally right. We shall not take your case, but will give you a little advice for which we will charge you nothing. You seem to be a sprightly, energetic man. We would advise you to try your hand at making six hundred dollars in some other way."

Lincoln believes there's a higher law than the standard of doing what is legally permissible. He tells his good friend Joshua Speed, "I have an irrepressible desire to live till I can be assured that the world is a little better for my having lived in it."

An acquaintance of Lincoln's has just become a justice of the peace, and asks him for some advice. Lincoln explains that justice is the collective wisdom of previous generations. When you try a case, Lincoln advises, ask yourself, what is fair, what is just, what is the right thing, and let those considerations guide your decision.

October 15, 1858. Alton, Illinois. A crowd of over five thousand people has gathered for the last debate between Lincoln and Stephen Douglas. Perhaps because it is their last debate that Lincoln is thinking about what it all means. All the thousands of words that have been spoken. The jokes, the thrusts, the parries, the crowds, the cheering. Is there something more important than just this election? Is there some principle? Something enduring? These are the questions that statesmen ask.

What follows is one of the most eloquent of all Lincoln's words:

"That is the issue. That is the issue that will continue in this country when these poor tongues of Judge Douglas and myself shall be silent. It is the eternal struggle between these two principles—right and wrong—throughout the world. They are the two principles that have stood face to face from the beginning of time, and will ever continue to struggle..."

Obama

During the run up to the vote on health care, Obama meets with his advisors every day. They tell him the poll numbers don't look good. They warn him to be a realist. But, according to the people Edward Klein interviews, every night Michelle and Barack talk about moral imperatives. She reminds him that he is there to do good, urges him to be bold.

Before he leaves the White House to become mayor of Chicago, Rahm Emmanuel, Obama's chief of staff, reminds him of political reality, tells Obama there is danger in risking everything on health care. Obama understands the chance he is taking. He knows what happened to presidents in the past who tried to get some version of universal health care. He knows what happened to the Clintons when they tried it. But he does it anyway.

Why does Obama push so hard for health care? Maybe it is because he wants to do what no other president has done. Maybe it's because of the battles that his mother had to fight with insurance companies when she was dying of cancer. Maybe it's because he wants to do something monumental during his presidency besides just keeping the shop open. Maybe he just wants to do what's right for millions of people.

Rahm is 100 percent loyal, but doesn't think big health care is the right call. He tells Richard Wolffe, "He [Obama] made a judgment based on 'This is a once-in-a-lifetime to get this done.' I can see, and I understand exactly, that this is the moment in time to make this political expenditure. That's what a president is supposed to do. And that's his strength."

Obama pays a price for his decision. Americans don't like to be told to do anything, and they certainly don't like to be told that they'll have to buy something, even if it's for their own good. And the individual mandate says you have to buy health insurance coverage, or pay a penalty.

The bill passes, and out come the "Don't Tread on Me" flags.

When the decides that the individual mandate is constitutional, Obama gives a short speech about doing the right thing:

I know there will be a lot of discussion today about the politics of all this, about who won and who lost. That's how these things tend to be viewed here in Washington. But that discussion completely misses the point. Whatever the politics, today's decision was a victory for people all over this country whose lives will be more secure because of this law and the Supreme Court's decision to uphold it.

V.
LINCOLN AND OBAMA AS PRESIDENTS

I'm glad you are cunning—as Lincoln
and Jackson were cunning.

– Carl Sandburg in a letter to
Franklin Roosevelt

LINCOLN AND OBAMA AS PRESIDENTS

POLICIES

A policy is to a government what a creed is to a church, what an agenda is to a meeting, what a contract is to a business. A policy is a vision, a core belief, a guideline, a set of priorities, a stated plan of action, a declaration of intent.

Taxes

"Taxes are what we pay for civilized society."

     – Oliver Wendell Holmes, Jr., US Supreme Court Justice

No American has ever thought more deeply about the nature of government that James Madison, who is sometimes called the Father of the Constitution, and the Father of the Bill of Rights. He and Alexander Hamilton and John Jay wrote a series of 85 newspaper articles in support of the Constitution—articles that became known as the *Federalist Papers*. Madison became the fourth president of the United States.

And what did this deeply knowledgeable American say is absolutely essential to our government? Taxes.

Here are James Madison's words: "The power of taxing people and their property is essential to the very existence of government."

Lincoln and Obama come to the same conclusion that Madison did. Any politician, who is not a charlatan, has to.

Lincoln

Lincoln needs money to prosecute the war, lots of it. It would be unthinkable for Lincoln to consider signing anything remotely like lobbyist Grover Norquist's no-tax-increase pledge, a lifetime pledge that virtually every Republican member of Congress has signed. A pledge that puts their brains into a kind of blind trust.

He asks Salmon Chase, his secretary of treasury, to find a way to raise funds. The first federal income tax in American history is initiated. It is a *federal* tax, it is collected at the income source as a withholding tax, and it is graduated or progressive; that is, the wealthy pay a higher percentage than those who make less. It is not a flat tax.

Three decades later, in 1895, the Supreme Court rules the federal income tax is unconstitutional. It is reinstated by the 16th Amendment, which is ratified in 1913: "The Congress shall have power to lay and collect taxes on incomes, from whatever source derived, without apportionment among the several States, and without regard to any census or enumeration."

Obama

Obama has a war to pay for. Actually two wars, which were begun on the watch of George W. Bush. One in Iraq and one in Afghanistan. The wars are enormously expensive. About three trillion dollars for the Iraq War alone. Nobody will ever know for sure, because much of the funding is for secret operations. And all along, the wars have not been paid for. Incredibly, much of the cost of the wars has been off the books.

The bills come due on Obama's watch, and members of Congress who once ardently supported the Iraq War have morphed into fiscal conservatives who now profess to be deeply concerned about the federal deficit.

The no-tax movement is at full stride. The carnage is everywhere. Cities are going into bankruptcy, slashing services, defaulting on pension plans, not paying creditors. School teachers are being fired at a time when the number of students is increasing. Is no one connecting the dots?

A computer expert tells me taxation is government theft. He uses the Internet, which was created at state universities and government research organizations, is dependent on a cell phone that gets its signal off a government-launched satellite, he attended public schools and is a graduate of a state university, he uses a public library, does his banking at a FDIC-insured bank, travels on the Interstate, loves our national parks, and his elderly parents are on Social Security—but does not see the contradiction.

The Tea Party comes into existence during the Obama administration. To be precise, the very first tea party was *not* a protest against taxation. It was a protest against taxation *without representation*. Americans today have representation at every level. When I explain this to a woman who invites me to participate in one of the first Tea Party rallies in Jacksonville, Florida, she politely brushes it aside. "We are not that historical," she says. "It's just a name."

Every American president, Democrat or Republican, has understood that taxation is essential to sound government.

Theodore Roosevelt, a Republican of wealth and privilege, supported a progressive income tax. He believed that the only safeguard the people have against big business is big government.

Another Roosevelt, he too of wealth and privilege, understood that the nation during the Great Depression faced two choices—violent revolution or peaceful reform. He chose reform. Many historians say the reforms of the 1930s saved American capitalism.

Yet FDR is called a socialist, a radical, a Communist. Rush Limbaugh—the man who many say has more power over the Republican Party than any other individual—has stated on the air that he lives for the day when everything FDR did will be undone.

Obama pushes reform. His focus is on health care for some thirty million Americans—10 percent of the people—who depend upon the charity of emergency rooms when they get hurt or sick.

Obama is called the same names that FDR was called.

One of the biggest challenges Obama faces is the Bush tax cuts. They are called the Bush tax cuts because George W. Bush, who inherited a huge surplus from Bill Clinton's administration, successfully persuaded Congress to cut taxes.

Members of Congress know how difficult it is to raise taxes once you cut them. So Congress at the time built in an automatic expiration. The tax cuts would automatically expire without anybody having to vote. A future Congress could just let the tax cuts expire, and when they did, taxes would rise slightly to what they were during the Clinton administration, which, incidentally, was a prosperous time in American history.

Obama is willing to let the Bush tax cuts expire for the richest Americans, who are doing very well. But he advocates keeping them at current levels for the poor and the middle class. He uses the word "share," and the right wing pounces on the expression. It's positive proof that Obama is a socialist. At the end of his first term, Obama wins this fight.

Obama talks about a "balanced" approach, which means budget cuts *and* increased revenue. Obama doesn't think ExxonMobil really needs government help, because it's been doing quite well. Indeed it has. Astonishingly well. In 2011, ExxonMobil reported more net profits than any business anywhere, any time in the history of the world. Yet it and other big oil companies have enough support in Congress to save their government subsidy.

Foreign Policy

Domestic policy is difficult for most presidents, but foreign policy is one area in which a president has considerable latitude. But both Lincoln and Obama are careful, cautious, anything but reckless.

Lincoln

Several incidents occur during the Civil War that could lead to a second or third war—wars with Spain, France, and England.

Lincoln has to restrain his secretary of state, which is ironic because Seward is the well-traveled, worldly wise man. Lincoln is the un-traveled, small-town lawyer.

One incident in particular, the Trent Affair, brings the US and Great Britain to the brink. An American ship stops a British ship in international waters, and arrests and removes two high-ranking Confederate diplomats who are aboard.

Threatening messages are exchanged, Parliament is in an uproar, and war fever is up in America. Lincoln weighs the costs, and realizes war with Great Britain will result in the unthinkable— international recognition of the Confederacy. If Great Britain recognizes the Confederacy, France, Spain, and Russia are sure to follow. That will be a disaster.

Lincoln tells Seward to tone down his messages; says he doesn't want "two wars on his hands at once."

Some accuse Lincoln of not standing up for America. But war is averted.

Obama

As soon as Obama secures the nomination, he leaves for visits to Afghanistan, Iraq, Jordan, Israel and the West Bank, France, England and Germany. Friendships are begun. For instance, after dinner in Amman, Jordan, King Abdullah II personally takes Obama to the airport. It is one of many such friendly experiences.

Obama wins the Nobel Peace Prize in 2009. His critics call it preposterous. They say he hasn't done anything. But Obama has done one thing. He has signaled that the go-it-alone foreign policy of the previous eight years is a thing of the past. And the rest of the world is heartened.

Leslie Gelb, former president of the Council on Foreign Relations, says no president has taken more personal control over foreign policy than Obama: "In other administrations, a lot of the decisions were made below the presidential level. But Obama shapes most policies. He takes pen to paper and writes decision papers...Obama always makes the calls on almost every subject, and with a degree of personal intensity."

Some begin to speak of what they call the Obama Doctrine. One journalist writes, "Generally speaking, it is accepted that a central part of such a doctrine would emphasize negotiation and collaboration rather than confrontation and unilateralism in international affairs."

Military Power

The two presidents are strategic and successful in their use of military power.

Lincoln

Victories are slow in coming during the Civil War. There are devastating defeats during the first two years. And then slowly the tide begins to turn. Vicksburg and Gettysburg, Lookout Mountain and Missionary Ridge, Mobile Bay and Nashville. And just in time for the presidential election, there's a stunning victory in Atlanta that turns everything around. The capture of Atlanta is followed by Sherman's March to the Sea, which military leaders here and abroad still marvel at.

Obama

So many al-Qaeda leaders are killed that Stephen Colbert quips that the president, "rather than sending prisoners to Gitmo, is taking the high road by sending them to their maker."

Obama ends the Iraq War, and Osama bin Laden is caught and killed in a daring raid deep inside Pakistan. The Libya campaign ends successfully, the result of a coalition of NATO powers. Obama's critics lampoon the strategy as "leading from behind."

Obama does not get much credit for Libya, but should. No American lives are lost, it's a team victory for NATO, and the dictator behind the Lockerbie bombing of Pan Am Flight 103 is gone.

There is one result. Fewer critics call Obama soft on terrorism. And even fewer listen to them.

The drone strikes, the dramatic killing of bin Laden, the relentless pursuit of terrorist leaders, and the defeat of Gaddafi in Libya make such criticisms sound silly to a lot of Americans.

Environmental Issues

Both are responsive to environmental issues. Lincoln, in 1864, signs a bill to protect the Mariposa Giant Sequoias and Yosemite Valley. Obama supports clean energy legislation and initiatives, winning endorsements from major environmental organizations.

Advocacy of Women's Rights

One of the great ironies of American history, and a sad and inexcusable one, is how slowly American women have achieved equality. Black men—former slaves, in fact—get the right to vote decades before black or white women do.

Americans boast of exceptionalism, but England was crowning queens centuries ago, and it chose a woman as prime minister three decades ago. The disparity in the way American men and women are treated has not been lost on Lincoln and Obama.

Lincoln

Almost a century before the 19th Amendment is ratified, Lincoln advocates women's suffrage. His support is muted, and oblique, and race-based, but it is there. When Lincoln is just 27, and a real novice at politics, he publishes his political views in a letter to the editor of *The Sangamo Journal* in Illinois. Here are Lincoln's words: "I go for all sharing the privileges of the government, who assist in sharing its burthens (burdens). Consequently I go for admitting all whites to the rights of suffrage, who pay taxes or bear arms (*by no means excluding females*)." [Italics, mine.]

Obama

The very first act of Congress that Obama signs into law is a women's issue law—the Lilly Ledbetter Fair Pay Act—which removes barriers that women face suing for equal pay. It is named for a woman who was denied the right to sue for equal pay because of an overly restrictive statute of limitations. In 2010, Obama tells an audience, "I didn't run for president so that the dreams of our daughters could be deferred or denied."

The Affordable Care Act prevents insurance companies from discriminating based on gender. Women will be able to receive preventive services without co-pays or deductibles. On August 1, 2012, approximately 47 million women become eligible for free access to mammograms, FDA-approved contraception techniques, HIV screening, and annual preventative health visits.

Mike Kelly, a Republican member of Congress, is not pleased by the new provisions. On national TV, Kelly says August 1, 2012 will live in infamy, comparing it to Pearl Harbor and 9/11.

Sympathy toward Immigrants

The American story is a tale of immigrants. In America's great cities, there have always been sections of town where you will not hear a word of English. The first language they speak are Dutch, German, Yiddish, Italian, Spanish, Arabic, Chinese, Hindi, Urdu, Korean, Amharic, Yoruba, Ibo and hundreds of other languages and dialects. But their children will learn the English language and American ways, and the process will continue. A Polish woman explains, the Germans tried to make Germans of us, and we remained Poles. The Americans do not care. We will soon become Americans.

Well, maybe. Not all Americans do not care, then or now. There are always some Americans who want to force the process, make it hard on the newcomer. In August 2012, the House of Representatives conducts a hearing on making English the official language of the United States, making it illegal to do business with the government in other languages. Its chances of becoming law are zero, but its supporters will tell their constituents back home that they have stood up for America.

Lincoln

The 1850s is a time of fierce nativist feelings, especially against Catholic immigrants. Lincoln writes to Joshua Speed: "I am not a Know-Nothing. That is certain. How could I be? How can anyone who abhors the oppression of Negroes be in favor of degrading classes of white people? Our progress in degeneracy appears to me to be pretty rapid. As a nation, we began by declaring that 'all men are created equal.' We now practically read it 'all men are created equal, except negroes.' When the Know-Nothings get control, it will read 'all men are created equal, except negroes, and foreigners, and Catholics.'"

The Homestead Act passes in 1862. It has a pro-immigrant component. Foreigners can get title to 160 acres if they work the land for five years, just like native-born Americans. Many accept the offer.

Germans immigrate to Nebraska from Russia, and introduce winter wheat. The descendants of those original homesteaders are still in Nebraska. When you drive through the farmland around Beatrice, and visit the Homestead National Monument, you will see golden blocks of winter wheat surrounded by a deep green sea of corn. It feels good to understand how this happened.

Lincoln spends his adult life around immigrants. Almost half of Springfield's population in the 1850s is immigrants, mainly Irish and Germans. Immigrants are a major factor in the war. Close to 200,000 Union soldiers are German-born.

Lincoln invests in a German newspaper. He makes a deliberate effort to promote officers from ethnic groups, in particular officers with German names. Today Lincoln's behavior would be called "politically correct," but he just wants to be inclusive. Lincoln understands why the founding fathers liked the phrase *e pluribus Unum,* "out of many one."

Obama

Like the 1850s, the twenty-first century is a time of anger directed at immigrants. It is not the Germans or the Irish now. Today, immigrant-haters focus mainly on Muslims and Latinos.

In this controversy, opponents of amnesty and immigration reform are insistent about immigrants obeying the letter of the law. Immigrants without papers are "illegals." Truth be told, American history is the history not just of immigrants, but "illegals."

The Proclamation of 1763 strictly forbade colonists from settling west of the Appalachians. In fact about 10,000 British troops served as a sort of border patrol.

Early Americans paid little attention to the law. They swarmed westward. Daniel Boone, the iconic frontiersman, in today's parlance, was really a smuggler of illegals. And some of those screaming loudest about today's illegals may be descendants of yesterday's illegals.

In 2012, Obama announces that the government will stop deporting the children of undocumented immigrants. He is thinking long-term. These children will grow up. Soon! The question is what will they be like when they grow up?

If they're treated right, and invested in properly, the children of today's illegal immigrants will become tomorrow's physicians and nurses, school teachers and firefighters, sailors and soldiers and pilots, judges and mayors and, one day, maybe president.

CRITICISM AND CONFLICTS

"Job Killers"

Lincoln

"Do you have any idea what a civil war will do to the economy of this city?" Fernando Wood, New York's mayor asks.

Wood has been thinking about taking New York out of the Union. He wants to keep on doing business with the South.

Wood is barely civil to Lincoln when Lincoln stops by for a visit on his way to be inaugurated. Wood lectures Lincoln that if he doesn't compromise with Southerners about expanding slavery into the West, grass will grow in the streets of America's great cities.

Lincoln replies that if he has anything to do with it, the only place grass will grow will be in meadows and pastures.

Lincoln is told that the great state of Georgia has voted not to wear any clothing made in northern mills. Lincoln replies, if Georgians wear just clothing made in Georgia mills, he thinks they will go around naked. Lincoln thinks it's worth making a trip down to Georgia just to see that sight.

Obama

Obama kills jobs, his foes say. He is pro-regulation, which is a real job killer. Forget about the BP oil spill in the Gulf. Regulation hurts American business. Besides, how can Americans compete with nations that let their industries exploit labor, and despoil the oceans, rivers and atmosphere?

Obama kills jobs because he is pro-tax. He is accused of punishing "job creators," a euphemism for rich people.

A *New Yorker* cartoon picks up that idea. A robber is holding a gun on an obviously well-off man. The robber is saying, "I'm really sorry to do this to a *job creator*."

Religious Views

The US Constitution forbids religious tests for holding public office. Here are the words: "No religious test shall ever be required as a qualification to any office or public trust under the United States."

These words may be in the Constitution, but the chances of an avowed atheist or a member of an out-of-favor religion becoming president are not great. It's always been this way. Alexis de Tocqueville writes in the 1830s, "Religion, which never intervenes directly in the government of American society, should (nevertheless) be considered as the first of their political institutions."

The big exception is Thomas Jefferson. Jefferson's opponents call him a pagan and an infidel. New England farm wives bury their Bibles because they hear that Jefferson will confiscate them. A pastor warns: "If Jefferson is elected, the Bible will be burned, the French 'Marseillaise' will be sung in Christian churches, and we may see our wives and daughters become the victims of legal prostitution."

Lincoln and Obama both must deal with attacks on their religious beliefs. Each has to make a public statement to reassure the public about their religion.

Lincoln

Even today, Lincoln's religious beliefs are a big question mark. People find proof that Lincoln is a skeptic, a deist, an agnostic, a Unitarian, a Trinitarian, a spiritualist, and a born-again Christian.

There is strong evidence that during his early years, Lincoln is a skeptic. The village of New Salem is a hotbed of radical thought, with known "free thinkers." New Salem has no church, but the writings of Tom Paine and Voltaire are discussed in the debating society. One man by the name of Jesse Fell who knew Lincoln then remembers that Lincoln "held opinions utterly at variance with what are usually taught in the churches," and adds that his views "would place Lincoln entirely outside the Christian pale." James Matheny, blaming the poet Robert Burns for Lincoln's views, says: "Burns helped Lincoln to be an infidel as I think—at least he found in Burns a like thinker and feeler." Matheny claims that "Holy Willie's Prayer is 'Lincoln's religion.'"

Robert Burn's famous satire mocks the idea that God chooses some people for heaven and others for hell, without regard for what the people do. Neither Lincoln nor Burns believe that doctrine, even though it is passionately preached from pulpits.

But a trace of that idea lingers. Lincoln never gets away from a fatalistic view of life. The Almighty rules over the world, Lincoln says again and again. He is fond of quoting, "There's a divinity that shapes our ends, rough-hew them how we may." He says "Man proposes, God disposes" in a speech at Baltimore's Sanitary Commission fair. This idea runs through the Second Inaugural Address.

Early on, Lincoln writes a skeptical essay along the lines of Thomas Paine's *Age of Reason*. Lincoln shows it to his friend Samuel Hill; Hill snatches the manuscript and tosses it into the fire. Several people recall the incident. Hill and other acquaintances give Lincoln this advice: a politician might survive in America if he is not a church member, but he cannot survive if he gets to be known as anti-religious.

Lincoln runs for Congress. Rumors begin to circulate about Lincoln's radical views. Of all the people in the world to run against, his opponent is a famous Methodist evangelist by the name of Peter Cartwright. Talk about a choice between God and the Devil!

Lincoln has a handbill printed. Here are some sentences from it:

> *FELLOW CITIZENS:*
> *A charge having got into circulation in some of*
> *the neighborhoods of this District, in substance*
> *that I am an open scoffer at Christianity, I have by*
> *the advice of some friends concluded to notice the*
> *subject in this form.*
>
> *That I am not a member of any Christian Church*
> *is true; but I have never denied the truth of the*
> *Scriptures; and I have never spoken with*
> *intentional disrespect of religion in general, or*
> *any denomination of Christians in particular... "*

Wayne Temple writes the definitive book on the subject of Lincoln's religion, and he gives his book this title, "Abraham Lincoln: From Skeptic to Prophet."

We know about the skeptic part. What about prophet?

By the time Lincoln reaches the White House, he is no longer a skeptic. He never loses his skeptical turn of mind, but he is no scoffer at religion.

Watch Lincoln being inaugurated. When the chief justice administers the oath of office, when the last word is spoken, Lincoln reaches over and kisses the Bible that the chief justice is holding.

He prays, and proclaims days of prayer and thanksgiving.

He memorizes verses from the Bible, and meditates on them. He writes down his musings.

He writes the Emancipation Proclamation but delays announcing it until he gets a providential sign. He gets one at the Battle of Antietam.

A minister of immense influence, Charles G. Finney, tells William Herndon, Lincoln's law partner, about a letter he wrote to Lincoln. Finney is president of what is now Oberlin College. Before coming to Oberlin, Finney had been a leading and innovative figure in a revival that spreads across several states.

Finney tells Herndon: "It would seem as if any man living soberly through the first two years [of the War] must've felt the divine presence very near. Lincoln did not, and it troubled me so that when he gave notice that, certain conditions failing, he would publish on 1 January a proclamation of emancipation, I wrote him a letter and begged him to treat the subject as if it were the Lord's business he was about. I don't know whether my letter did any good, or whether the Lord did in his own way, but when the paper was published, I found the words I wanted…That was the first time."

Lincoln attends church. It is usually a Presbyterian church. The Presbyterians are closest doctrinally to the Calvinistic beliefs his parents held. Lincoln's parents are called "hard-shell" Baptists, not "free-will" Baptists.

Lincoln says he will join a church if he ever finds one with just two requirements: One—Thou shalt love the Lord thy God with all thy heart and soul, and Two—Thou shalt love thy neighbor as thy self.

The churches Lincoln is acquainted with have many more than two requirements, and they are not just doctrinal issues. Dancing is a big issue at the two Presbyterian churches in Springfield. Thou shalt not dance. Lincoln attends dances, although Mary Todd tells her friends that he dances "in the worst possible way."

Lincoln never makes a public confession or is baptized or joins a church or takes communion.

What does Lincoln believe? The reports differ wildly.

Mary Lincoln tells Herndon that her husband was "naturally religious."

David Homer Bates, who often observed Lincoln at the telegraph office in the War Department, states that "if love be the fulfilling of the law of Christ, Abraham Lincoln in his day and generation was the nearly perfect human example of the operation of that law."

Dr. William Jayne, a Springfield neighbor and close friend, says, "It is now beyond the realm of controversy that Lincoln loved, honored and revered Almighty God."

Another friend Noah Brooks goes farther than that: "I am glad to say that I have a firm belief in Mr. Lincoln's saving knowledge of Christ. He talked always of Christ, his cross, his atonement."

Ward Hill Lamon, one of Lincoln's closest friends, disagrees with Brooks: "Never in all that time did he let fall from his lips or pen an expression which remotely implied the slightest faith in Jesus as the Son of God and the Savior of men."

Wayne Temple, who has studied Lincoln's beliefs meticulously for decades, and has read the original documents, concludes, "Lincoln did read the Bible and prayed constantly, but it is extremely doubtful that he talked openly to anybody about Christ's atonement for man's sins, etc. Lincoln spoke mainly of God and to God."

Obama

"Lincoln was a Christian," a man in Lake Mary, Florida tells me. "He was not like what we've got in the White House now."

The man loves Lincoln, is suspicious of Obama. He thinks Obama might be a Muslim.

On February 21, 2012, the featured guest on MSNBC'S *Morning Joe* is Rev. Franklin Graham, president and CEO of the Billy Graham Evangelistic Association, and son of the renowned Rev. Billy Graham.

Franklin Graham is asked if he believes Obama is a Christian. "I think you have to ask President Obama," he replies. "I cannot answer that question for anybody."

He adds that because Obama's father was a Muslim, "under Islamic law, the Muslim world sees Barack Obama as a Muslim." Franklin does not mention that Obama has spent virtually no time with his father.

He is asked, "Do you believe Rick Santorum is a Christian?" Santorum, a Roman Catholic, is a GOP presidential candidate at the time. Graham replies, "I think so."

A panel member asks, "How do you know, if the standard is *only the person knows what's in him*...Why is it different for Rick Santorum?"

"Well, because his values are so clear on moral issues," Graham replies. "No question about it. I just appreciate the moral stances he takes on things. He comes from a Catholic faith…I think he's a man of faith."

Franklin Graham is asked if Mitt Romney is a Christian.

"Most Christians would not recognize Mormons as part of the Christian faith. They believe in Jesus Christ. They have a lot of other things they believe in too, that we don't accept, theologically." Then Graham adds, "I like him…He would be a good president…He's a sharp guy."

There is outrage about Graham's comments. The interview begins to be called "infamous" on the Internet. Graham apologizes: "I regret any comments I have ever made which may have cast any doubt on the personal faith of our president, Mr. Obama."

Graham explains that what Obama believes about traditional marriage and abortion has helped him make a decision. "My objection to President Obama is built on his policy positions and not on his religion or faith. For example, I believe his positions on abortion and on traditional marriage are in direct conflict with God's standards as set forth in Scripture."

Graham's explanation leaves one question unanswered. What does Graham mean by *traditional* marriage? Which tradition? Franklin Graham is deeply versed in Scripture, and certainly knows that the Biblical patriarchs Abraham, Isaac and Jacob, plus the great kings David and Solomon, had multiple wives. Surely Graham does not mean that kind of traditional marriage.

That statement makes one think about Lincoln's saying that he would join a church if he ever found one that has just two requirements: Love the Lord with all your heart; and Love your neighbor as yourself.

In Springfield, in Lincoln's time, the big issue was dancing. Now it's abortion and traditional marriage.

That interview tells a lot about the controversy over President Obama's religion.

This much is known.

Obama is a member of a Christian church, has made a confession of faith, and has been baptized.

Lincoln, you remember, never joined a church or made a confession of faith, nor was he baptized or took communion.

Obama speaks of accepting Jesus Christ as his Savior, which is a generally acceptable statement of faith among evangelicals.

Some claim that Lincoln said this too; but Robert Lincoln, his son, and some of Lincoln's closest friends, don't recall ever hearing it.

Obama attends church services. So did Lincoln.

What do critics say?

They say Obama is really a Muslim, that his membership in a Christian church is a smoke screen for his true belief.

Lincoln is accused of being an infidel, but there is no record that Lincoln is ever accused of being a Muslim.

A thoughtful man in Illinois, who believes Obama is a Muslim, reminds me that Obama grew up in Indonesia where he was indoctrinated in Muslim schools. He's heard that the schools that Obama attended are *madrassas,* Muslim seminaries.

A check of the record shows that Obama was in Hawaii for kindergarten plus grades five through twelve. That leaves grades one through four for the possible Muslim indoctrination in Indonesia. The first three grades are in a school named St. Francis of Assisi Catholic School, which does not sound like the name of a Muslim seminary.

If the man is correct, Obama was indoctrinated into the Islamic faith during the fourth grade, when he was nine years old.

CNN dispatches senior international correspondent John Vause to Jakarta to check out just how radical the school is that Obama attended when he was a fourth-grader. What Obama learned in the fourth grade is that important.
Vause has seen *madrassas* in Pakistan, but he says this is not one. It is a public school with a mixed student body. There are a lot of Christians and Buddhists.

There is no parallel here with Lincoln. We can say with absolute certainty that Lincoln never had to explain what he studied in the fourth grade, because Lincoln never went to the fourth grade.

Critics complain that Obama does not go to church often enough. A blog titled "Thoughts from a Conservative Mom" reports in December 2011 that the Obamas have attended church just 10 times, but that he has played Sunday golf 88 times.

In comparison, Lincoln's attendance at church was not all that regular either. But Lincoln did not play golf.

Obama has done nothing to match Texas Governor Rick Perry, who called for a prayer rally, which would help him decide whether to run for president. *The Guardian* runs this account: "It was billed as a day of prayer and fasting to halt America's national decline, and about thirty thousand answered the call, flooding into Houston's Reliant Stadium for a seven-hour marathon which blended Christian revivalism with hard-headed electoral campaigning."

A few days later, Perry announces his decision. He will run. Perry briefly surges to the head of the GOP pack. It looks like the Lord is with him; but then Perry begins to falter. In a big debate, Perry can't remember which departments of the federal government he will eliminate. Where is the Lord when you really need him? Perry drops out of the race. No prayer rally is announced to help with that decision.

Ironically, it is Obama's membership in a church that almost destroys him politically. It is the Trinity United Church of Christ, a mega-church in Chicago, with 6,000 members. Its pastor is Jeremiah Wright.

ABC News runs a story in 2007 with excerpts of some of Wright's sermons, including Wright saying that the 9/11 attacks are "America's chickens coming home to roost." Wright says, "Not God bless America, but God damn America."

Meanwhile, less is made of a TV show that airs on the Christian Broadcasting Network, CBN. Two famous religious leaders—Pat Roberson and Rev. Jerry Falwell—are discussing 9/11. Falwell says the attack may have happened because of moral decay. He specifically mentions the ACLU, abortionists, feminists, gays and the People for the American Way who should share in the blame. Pat Robertson agrees.

One way to look at this episode is to see all three of these religious leaders—Jeremiah Wright and Pat Robertson and Jerry Falwell—as part of a venerable theological tradition.

Catastrophes and disasters have long been interpreted as God's judgment—eclipses, plagues of locusts, droughts, defeats by the enemy have been associated with divine displeasure throughout history. Jewish prophets explained that the children of Israel are cursed—God damned, if you will—because of their sins.

There's a word for this kind of sermon—*Jeremiad,* as in the Old Testament prophet Jeremiah. No pun intended. Now hear the words of Jeremiah: "Because of the abominations which you have committed; therefore is your land a desolation, and an astonishment, and a curse, without an inhabitant as at this day."

And not just Old Testament prophets, like Jeremiah. Christian ministers have preached the same message about the bubonic plague, invasions, and the great fires of London and Chicago.

Even Lincoln adopts this theme in his great Second Inaugural Address: "Yet, if God wills that it [the Civil War] continue until all the wealth piled by the bondsman's two hundred and fifty years of unrequited toil shall be sunk, and until every drop of blood drawn with the lash shall be paid by another drawn with the sword, as was said three thousand years ago, so still it must be said that the judgments of the Lord are true and righteous altogether."

Obama's critics do not interpret Jeremiah Wright as part of this grand tradition. Wright is outrageous, unpatriotic. Wright would have fared much better had he said God damn the People for the American Way, or God damn the ACLU.

Obama gives a speech distancing himself from Wright's views. Obama sees it as a teachable moment, and calls his speech "A More Perfect Union."

Some compare Obama's speech with the one that John F. Kennedy gave to a group of Protestant pastors in Houston. "I believe in an America where the separation of church and state is absolute," Kennedy tells the preachers, "where no Catholic prelate would tell the President—should he be Catholic—how to act, and no Protestant minister would tell his parishioners for whom to vote ... For while this year it may be a Catholic against whom the finger of suspicion is pointed," Kennedy warns, "in other years it has been—and may someday be again—a Jew, or a Quaker, or a Unitarian, or a Baptist."

Kennedy's speech puts the matter of a Catholic president to rest.

But Obama's speech does not have the same quieting effect— even though he calls Wright's comments "inflammatory and appalling." Even though he tells the editorial board of the *Chicago Tribune*, "He's like your uncle who says things you profoundly disagree with, but he's still your uncle."

Jeremiah Wright says on TV he knows why Obama is saying all those hurtful things about him. It's "political posturing."

Obama replies: "The person that I saw yesterday was not the person that I met twenty years ago. His comments were not only divisive and destructive, but I believe that they end up giving comfort to those who prey on hate. And I believe that they do not portray accurately the perspective of the black church. They certainly don't portray accurately my values and beliefs. And if Reverend Wright thinks that that's political posturing, as he put it, then he doesn't know me very well."

Obama resigns his membership in Wright's church.

More than four years after ABC originally aired the Jeremiah Wright material, the issue is still bubbling on the right. A few Obama haters think the brew might still have some kick left in it.

Obama tells Richard Wolffe, "You look at somebody like Lincoln who starts off, as far as we can tell, deeply skeptical of religion, but a powerfully moral person who as he finds himself in the midst of history and a potential cataclysm feels it necessary to hang on to a more explicit belief in Providence and faith. And so that resonates with me. I think that there's a place where the more seriously you take the world, and the more you find yourself struggling with good and evil or, you know, the great moral questions of the day, the more you have to fall back on some sort of North Star."

That sounds a lot like Lincoln, who says, "I must keep some standard of principle fixed within myself."

Patriotism

Opposing a war that is underway is almost always fatal to a politician. War has a momentum of its own that makes it virtually unstoppable.

Ask John Kerry or George McGovern about that. Both ran for president, but their opponents effectively used their anti-war stance against them.

Lincoln and Obama feel its sting, but somehow manage to survive. In fact, Lincoln and Obama are the only two American politicians who outspokenly oppose an American war, who later manage to become president.

Lincoln

Lincoln, along with most Whigs in Congress, opposes the War with Mexico. He makes an impassioned speech on the floor of the House denouncing it, says the United States provoked it. Lincoln votes to fund the war, but that does not save him. Herndon writes to tell him how unpopular his anti-war views are. Back home, people start calling Lincoln "the Benedict Arnold of Illinois."

When General U.S. Grant writes his memoirs, he makes an observation about what happens to politicians who oppose wars: "Experience proves that the man who obstructs a war in which his nation is engaged, no matter right or wrong, occupies no enviable place in life or history. Better for him, individually, to advocate 'war, pestilence and famine' than to act as obstructionist to a war already begun."

Lincoln learns the truth of Grant's observation. After his opposition to the Mexican War, there's little chance he can live it down. You can hear people telling Lincoln that he is a fool, that we got all of Texas, California and everything in-between for virtually nothing. Keep your scruples to yourself, Abraham Lincoln, and get back to doing what you know something about.

Lincoln returns to doing law in earnest for many long, obscure years. What brings him out of political exile is the Dred Scott decision, and the resulting turmoil in Kansas. Soon Lincoln is involved in political skirmishes, then the big debates with his old foe, the US Senator from Illinois Stephen Douglas. Those debates with Douglas, and his strong showing in the election of 1858, revive Lincoln's political career.

Obama

It's 2002. Obama is an Illinois Senator, but he is not well known outside Illinois. He opposes the Iraq War, expressing his feelings this way: "I don't oppose all wars. What I oppose is a dumb war."

Four years later, he is asked about those comments: "Look, when I spoke out against going to war in Iraq in 2002, Bush was at sixty to sixty-five percent in the polls. I was putting my viability as a US Senate candidate at risk. It looks now like an easy thing to do, but it wasn't then."

When Obama runs for president, his opponents remind voters about his anti-war sentiments.

And there's more. They take note of the fact that Obama bows and scrapes before world leaders. Obama apologizes for America's alleged misdeeds, as though he does not truly believe in American exceptionalism. And one other thing, Obama doesn't always wear an American-flag lapel pin.

"This is not a man who sees America the way you and I see America," says John McCain's running mate, Sarah Palin.

But Obama can counter-punch.

John McCain chooses "Country First" for his campaign theme.

Unanswerable?

Not really.

Obama waits to land his punch until Thursday night August 28, 2008 at Invesco Field, home of the Denver Broncos. It's the 45th anniversary of MLK's historic "I Have a Dream" speech. Over 90,000 people are there, and millions more are watching worldwide.

Obama says, "I've got news for you, John McCain…We **ALL** put country first."

The people in the stadium go wild.

Extremism

One way to destroy an American politician is to say the politician has extremist views, or associates with people who do. During the 1960s, the White Citizens Councils put up billboards all over the South with a photo of MLK surrounded by radicals and extremists.

The tactic works against politicians left and right. LBJ paints an extremist label on Barry Goldwater. LBJ runs an attack ad. A horrifying nuclear explosion destroys a daisy-counting little girl. Then comes the message: *The world is too dangerous a place to risk voting for an extremist.*

Goldwater is annihilated at the polls in 1964. He wins just six states—his home state of Arizona, plus the Deep South states. But something significant happens. Goldwater does what Lincoln and the Republicans could never do. He carries the Deep South.

The tactic is used against a leftie—Senator George McGovern. McGovern is portrayed as an extremist, as un-American, as someone who wants to stop the Vietnam War.

In 1972, McGovern carries just one state—Massachusetts, the state of his running-mate Sargent Shriver. The other 49 states go for Richard Nixon.

George Bush Sr. uses the tactic against Michael Dukakis, in the 1988 presidential campaign. Bush calls Dukakis "a card-carrying member of the ACLU." It's silly, but it works with people who don't know what the "C" stands for in ACLU. They don't know it stands for "American Civil Liberties Union." It could mean Communist. They do know what "card carrying" means.

Lincoln

Lincoln in his youth pals around with radicals. Old timers recall that Lincoln boarded with a man named Jack Kelso. Kelso is a well-read man, versed in Shakespeare and Robert Burns. He can quote them by heart by the hour. Kelso and Lincoln fish together, recite poetry together, discuss politics together. Kelso is known as the village philosopher. They both are members of the debating society. And they both are acquainted with the writings of Tom Paine.

Paine, incidentally, is an extremist; he is a wanted man in some places. If you are an aristocrat in the 1770s, Tom Paine is your counterpart to the 1980s radical Bill Ayers. Paine never detonates a bomb that we know of, but Paine writes "Common Sense," which detonates the American Revolution. John Adams writes, "Without the pen of the author of *Common Sense*, the sword of Washington would have been raised in vain."

Lincoln spends a lot of time thinking and talking about Paine's ideas. For several years at least, Lincoln believes what Tom Paine wrote.

Lincoln eventually moves into the orbit of another kind of extremist, the abolitionist. Lincoln's law partner Billy Herndon is one. You need to know that in the 1830s and 1840s and 1850s, abolitionists are a tiny minority, located mainly in New England. They are disliked in the North and hated in the South because slave owners are afraid they will spark a slave revolt. Abolitionists who venture into the South know they risk their lives. Killings occur even in the North. Elijah Lovejoy, who is editor of an abolitionist paper in Alton, Illinois, is shot by a mob in 1837.

Lincoln is opposed to slavery, but he is not an abolitionist. He is cautious, a moderate, a reformer. But Herndon is nudging Lincoln toward the left. Herndon subscribes to abolitionist publications, and makes sure they come to the office. He signs Lincoln up as a Republican when that party begins to form.

Herndon later says that this is the turning point in Lincoln's life. Another one. "Never did a man change as Lincoln did from that hour." Herndon writes. "No sooner had he planted himself right on the slavery question, than his whole soul seemed burning. He blossomed right out." Herndon's description of what happens to Lincoln sounds very much like the way sages and mystics talk about aligning one's self with the universe.

Lincoln may be "planted right on the slavery question," as Herndon puts it, but Lincoln is still pragmatic. At the time of his inauguration, Lincoln is convinced, like most Americans at the time, that abolitionist extremists do more harm than good.

During his four years in office, Lincoln seems to surprise himself, doing what he has to do, doing what he gets to do, one day at a time.

War does have a momentum of its own, but war has consequences that often cannot be predicted. Lincoln observes that if the people across the Potomac had behaved themselves, all the radical things that are occurring—slaves emancipated, former slaves bearing arms for the Union—that wouldn't be happening.

Radical times can produce radical decisions in the White House.

And so we come to the end of 1864. The tough re-election battle has been fought and won. The end of the war is in sight.

Congratulatory messages pour in to the White House. One of them is from London, personally written by none other than Karl Marx. Marx is living in London, obscure and poor. He spends his time writing books and pamphlets that few bother to read. It will not be until years after his death that billions of people will live under governments that call themselves Marxist.

Marx is very much aware of Lincoln. The London papers run stories constantly about the war. Marx occasionally writes dispatches as foreign correspondent for the *New York Tribune*. His close friend and co-author of "The Communist Manifesto"—Frederick Engels— is a cotton-mill owner. Engels certainly knows what is happening in the Cotton States.

Marx personally writes his message to Lincoln in November 1864 on behalf of the Central Council of the International Workingmen's Association. Marx begins the letter:

> *Sir:*
> *We congratulate the American people upon your re-election by a large majority. If resistance to the Slave Power was the reserved watchword of your first election, the triumphant war cry of your re-election is Death to Slavery.*

Lincoln does not answer personally, but the American ambassador in London, Charles Francis Adams, Sr., does, with a guarded reply. The United States does not want to publicly embrace a reactionary union. But neither does it want to alienate workers. The workers in the mills have helped keep the British Empire from recognizing the Confederacy.

Here are two paragraphs from the ambassador's reply. Incidentally it sounds very modern, does it not?

> *I am directed to inform you that the address of the Central Council of your Association, which was duly transmitted through this Legation to the President of the United [States], has been received by him.*

> *So far as the sentiments expressed by it are personal, they are accepted by him with a sincere and anxious desire that he may be able to prove himself not unworthy of the confidence which has been recently extended to him by his fellow citizens*

and by so many of the friends of humanity and
progress throughout the world.

Marx would have no way of knowing how such a letter would be perceived in the US today if the most famous Communist in the world were to personally write a letter to the president. You can see the headline: "Obama's signature program praised by world's top Communist." In Congress, there would be calls for impeachment.

Politicians, or pretty girls, cannot always choose who like them.

Some Marxists and Catholic-hating Know-Nothings liked Lincoln. And some Black Muslims like Obama. But that does not make Lincoln a Know-Nothing or Obama a Black Muslim.

Obama

Obama makes no attempt to hide his exposure to radical thought during the two years he spends at Occidental College. It's there for everybody to read in *Dreams from My Father*.

Occidental College is a liberal arts college, founded in 1867 by a group of Presbyterian clergymen in the Eagle Rock community near Los Angeles. Over the years, a number of its students become Rhodes scholars and win Fulbright fellowships. It prides itself on its diverse student body, the range of thought students are exposed to.

He evolves into someone who is anything but extreme. He recognizes the contribution that people who are considered extreme in their time make to American history. But he knows that, neither by temperament or inclination, nor by training or practice, is he one of them.

Obama muses: "It has not always been the pragmatist, the voice of reason, or the force of compromise that has created the conditions for liberty. Knowing this, I can't summarily dismiss those possessed of similar certainty today—the anti-abortion activist, the animal-rights activist who raids a laboratory—no matter how deeply I disagree with their views, I am robbed [of] even the certainty of uncertainty—for sometimes absolute truths may well be absolute."

Indeed, nothing Obama has done as president is radical. After the Affordable Care Act (ACA) passes in the House, Obama tells journalists, "This isn't radical reform, but it is major reform. This legislation will not fix everything that ails our healthcare system but it moves us decisively in the right direction. This is what change looks like."

The ACA certainly is *not* radical. It requires Americans to purchase health insurance from *private* companies. How can that be called socialism? A lot of Americans think it would be a good idea just to lower the age requirements for Medicare. Medicare-for-all is the idea. Many conservatives like that idea, too. But the ACA doesn't go that far.

Information like this does not satisfy Obama's critics. They don't want you to forget that Obama once associated with radicals. They plow that field until there's not a weed left.

As the campaign heats up in the summer of 2012, Mitt Romney begins to insert the word "foreign" into his speeches whenever he mentions Obama: "He [Obama] disparages success, and wants to lead us down a path that's *foreign* to us." And there are throwaway lines: "This is something foreign."

Using the word *foreign* is a not-too-subtle way of sending a message that Obama is not one of us. It's virtually the same thing as saying "you people," or calling an individual an outsider, not one of us, an other.

Newt Gingrich, the philosopher-historian of the Republican Party, adds luster to that assessment. He comments: "What if [Obama] is so outside our comprehension, that only if you understand Kenyan, anti-colonial behavior, can you begin to piece together his actions? That is the most accurate, predictive model for his behavior."

It is true that Obama spent an entire month with his Kenyan father in Hawaii, when Obama was ten years old. Obama never sees his father again. But you can well imagine Obama and his father spending many an hour together in long, intense discussions about neocolonialism and radical politics.

If you go to Monticello, Thomas Jefferson's estate in Virginia, you will see an obelisk with Jefferson's epitaph inscribed on it. Before he died, Jefferson left directions about what he wanted said. *Write the following*, he instructed, and not a word more:

Here was buried
Thomas Jefferson
Author of the Declaration of American
Independence
of the Statute of Virginia for religious freedom
Father of the University of Virginia

Of the latter accomplishment—the University of Virginia—Jefferson writes: "This institution will be based on the illimitable freedom of the human mind. *For here we are not afraid to follow truth wherever it may lead, nor to tolerate any error so long as reason is left free to combat it.*"

No wonder Lincoln loved Thomas Jefferson.

Jefferson would never think of criticizing someone for exposing himself to radical, extremist thought, especially since Jefferson did it himself.

Views on Race

Both men are attacked for their views on race. Foes call Lincoln supporters "black Republicans" and "blacks." Obama's foes say that he "plays the race card."

Lincoln

At the time that Lincoln becomes president, his views on race are still evolving. And he has a long way to go. He hates slavery, and is willing to do everything in his power to keep it from spreading. He believes that blacks are protected under the Constitution, unlike his Democratic challenger Stephen Douglas or Chief Justice Roger Taney.

Lincoln thinks one good solution to the race problem is racial separatism—for blacks to return to Liberia, or perhaps to move to Central America or Santo Domingo. He tries to sell black leaders on the idea, but gets virtually no takers.

At first he resists arming black soldiers, but eventually comes around to thinking it's a good idea. By the end of the war, he is heaping praise on black warriors, specifically mentioning their bravery and sacrifice. He considers them essential to the war effort. Take them away, and give them to the enemy, Lincoln says, "and we can no longer maintain the contest."

Lincoln vows he will not abandon them: "If they stake their lives for us, they must be prompted by the strongest motive—even the promise of freedom. And the promise being made, must be kept."

Lincoln does not believe in racial equality early on. It is painful today to read some of his statements on the subject. The radicals of his party are far, far ahead of him on this score.

But Lincoln is growing and learning.

In 1864 Lincoln requests a meeting with Frederick Douglass, the famous former slave, social reformer and writer. During their meeting, the president is informed that the governor of Connecticut has arrived for his appointment.

Lincoln sends word, "Tell Governor Buckingham to wait. I want to have a long talk with my friend Frederick Douglass."

Years later, when Douglass writes his autobiography, he states, "This was probably the first time in the history of this Republic when its chief magistrate found occasion or disposition to exercise such an act of impartiality between persons so widely different in their positions and supposed claims upon his attention."

Lincoln may not be there yet, but he is getting closer.

An event about a year later tells its own story about Lincoln's journey. A glittering throng has crowded into the White House for a reception following the inauguration.

Frederick Douglass arrives at the door. Two policemen grab him, but he manages to bolt away. Once inside the hall, he is seized by two other policemen who begin to physically carry him out. Douglass cries out to a guest, "Please tell the president that Fred Douglass is here."

In less than a minute, word comes that the president wants to see him, and Douglass is escorted into the East Room. Here is what happens next:

"I could not have been more than ten feet from him when Mr. Lincoln saw me; his countenance lighted up, and he said in a voice which was heard all around; 'Here comes my friend Douglass.'

"As I approached him he reached out his hand, gave me a cordial shake, and said: 'Douglass, I saw you in the crowd today listening to my inaugural address. There is no man's opinion that I value more than yours; what do you think of it?' I said: 'Mr. Lincoln, I cannot stop here to talk with you, as there are thousands waiting to shake you by the hand'; but he said again: 'What did you think of it?' I said: 'Mr. Lincoln, it was a sacred effort.'

'I am glad you liked it,' he said. That was the last time I saw him to speak with him."

Six weeks later, Lincoln is buried.

Obama

In April 1968, racial rioting erupts in Washington, D.C. just after the assassination of Martin Luther King, Jr. Angry crowds, sometimes as large as 20,000, surge through the streets, trash and torch entire blocks, overwhelm the police.

Federal troops are sent in. Over 13,000 of them. Marines set up machine guns on the steps of the Capitol. An Army unit guards the White House. Rioters get within two blocks before they are turned back. It's the worst urban violence America has seen since the Civil War.

Americans discover that the social contract is more fragile than some had supposed.

Who would have thought then that a little over a generation later a peaceful crowd would gather to watch the inauguration of a black president? Many in this throng of tens of thousands are too young to remember the frightening days of the 1960s. Most don't even know it happened.

Obama takes the oath of office not far from where the Marines mounted their machine guns.

Obama's election stuns white bigots, and dismays fiery, old-time black radicals who preached that you can't ever trust Whitey. They don't have much of a message any more. Most blacks realize that this couldn't have happened without millions of white votes, whites who voted for a black man instead of a white man. Election night there are thousands of victory parties. Blacks and whites embracing, some shedding tears of joy.

Sociologists call Obama's victory a tipping point in American race relations. Even radical white right-wingers call a truce. They don't like Obama, some of them say, but he is president and deserves respect. They will salute the uniform, not the man. Their goodwill lasts several days. Then it's back to business as usual. The attacks resume.

In 2012 Obama expresses sympathy to the parents of Trayvon Martin, a black youth killed in an incident that attracts national attention. Obama says, "If I had a son, he would look like Trayvon...I can only imagine what these parents are going through, and when I think about this boy, I think about my own kids." Obama does not blame anyone, but his expression of sympathy is called racist by diehard critics. Most Americans read it as one parent expressing sympathy to another.

Relations with the Military

The founding fathers deliberately chose to place a civilian—the president—at the very top of the military chain of command. They knew about Caesar, and wanted no military dictator here.

And therein lies an inherent problem of troubling importance. There is a built-in-conflict when a president with no real military experience gives orders to generals and admirals. A civilian leader is not fluent in their special language, and may not understand their point of view. It must be difficult for some battle-hardened veterans to be ordered around by someone who has never seen combat.

Generals and admirals have the power to intimidate. The buildings, forts and bases intimidate. So do the crisp salutes, the rows of ribbons and medals on generals' and admirals' chests.

And presidents do get intimidated. It happens in presidency after presidency. One reason history repeats itself with presidents is because of the inherent conflict between the president and the military chain of command.

Lincoln

Dealing with the military is one of Lincoln's worst nightmares. And it is not the kind of nightmare that you wake up from, and you say, "I'm glad that was just a dream." It is an every day, every night nightmare, and it is not just a dream.

The first general-in-chief that Lincoln has to deal with is Winfield Scott, hero of the Mexican War. He's nicknamed "Old Fuss and Feathers." Not to be taken lightly, Scott is sensitive to slights, easily offended, speaks of himself in the third person. You can get some idea of the man by looking at his statue at Scott Circle in Washington.

Lincoln is disappointed in Scott. The general is loyal, but old and ill, too heavy and feeble even to mount a horse.

The president knows he will have to find good generals. Unfortunately, many of them, including Robert E. Lee, are now with the Confederates.

Lincoln soon settles on a general by the name of George B. McClellan. McClellan is young, a West-Point-trained engineer who's immensely popular with the troops. The press calls McClellan "young Napoleon." But unlike Napoleon, the man won't fight. He's better at drilling troops than winning battles. Lincoln eventually says of McClellan, he's a good engineer, but his specialty is *stationary* engines.

Lincoln repeatedly urges McClellan to be more aggressive. McClellan won't do it, is discourteous, views Lincoln with contempt, is insubordinate and disloyal.

Lincoln keeps McClellan on because he doesn't think he can do any better, plus the general is a member of the other political party. Lincoln desperately needs bi-partisan support for the war effort.

Lincoln eventually fires McClellan. Actually fires him twice. Most military historians think he should have done it sooner.

John M. Winchell, who is a member of the Washington staff of *The New York Times,* is meeting with Lincoln. Lincoln tells Winchell in confidence that he has no confidence in the plans of his military advisors.

Winchell asks, "Mr. President, if you disagree with the movements that are proposed, why do you permit them to be made?"

Lincoln answers, "Because I cannot prevent it.'

"But you are Commander-in-Chief."

"My dear Sir, I am as powerless as a private citizen to shape the military plans of the government. I have my generals and my war department, and my subordinates are supposed to be more capable than I am to decide what movements shall or shall not be taken...I tell you that sometimes when I reflect on the management of our forces, I am tempted to despair. My heart goes clear down into my boots."

When Winchell tells about this conversation a decade later, he says he is still astonished at Lincoln's admission of how powerless he was with his military.

Lincoln has great resolve, and he is not easily intimidated. He checks out books on military strategy from the Library of Congress. He educates himself so that he will know what's happening, will be able to ask good questions, will understand what to look for in a military leader. He eventually finds good generals and admirals, but it takes Lincoln time and a lot of sleepless nights before he does.

Obama

Obama's dealings with the military sound very much like Lincoln's.

Lincoln needs the support of Democrats.

Obama needs the support of Republicans.

Both have top generals who are authors of celebrated books on military strategy—for Lincoln, General Henry Halleck; and for Obama, General David Petraeus. Both must deal with senators who grandstand their own ideas about how the war should be prosecuted. All you need to do is substitute the names of the senators. Their words are almost identical.

Both must deal with rivalries among generals and admirals, among branches of the armed forces, between civilian and military advisors.

Some officers try to play Obama the same way military officers tried to play Lincoln. They always want more troops, and never lack a justification for their requests. They inflate estimates of needs and successes. All you need to do is substitute the names of the military leaders. Their words are almost identical, too.

But there is a big difference. In Lincoln's day, the military is tiny. Americans then were nervous about a standing army. Today the military is gigantic, deeply established, well-funded, and hard-wired with Congress and defense contractors. Eisenhower called it a "military industrial-complex," and warned the nation about it.

Let a president threaten it, and an enormous propaganda machine cranks up that can be overwhelming. Literally millions of jobs and billions of dollars in contracts are affected.

When the president makes known his decision about a military matter, few in the public know about the long hours, the intense debates, the dangerous path that led to the words the president uses.

Americans are fond of blaming military failures on politicians. It is so easy to beat up on politicians.

But politicians are the ones who have to go to the voters and persuade them to pay for the wars, the $400 million-dollar planes, the medical costs of the returning wounded. The politicians have to explain why schools and highways won't get built, and why the deficit is so large.

Presidents are politicians, and that is the political reality the president must take into account when the military insists that unless they get at least 40,000 more troops in Afghanistan—and the price of that deployment will be maybe $900 billion, not to mention the cost in blood—that if the president doesn't agree with their requests, well, America will lose the war. And it will be on your hands, Mr. President.

If you read Bob Woodward's meticulous reporting in *Obama's Wars,* you understand why making a decision about how many troops to give a general is so perilous for the president.

Woodward mentions a military advisor who tells the president, "I don't see how you can defy your military chain here, because if you tell General McChrystal, I got your assessment; but I've chosen to do something else, you're going to probably have to replace him. You can't tell him, just do it my way, thanks for your hard work, do it my way; and then where does that stop?"

Woodward spells out where it might stop. "Not only McChrystal, but General Petraeus, and Secretary of Defense Gates might go—an unprecedented toppling of the military high command. Perhaps no president could weather that."

Woodward quotes Leon Panetta, then Director of the CIA, later Secretary of Defense: "No Democratic president can go against military advice, especially if he has asked for it … So just do it, do what they say."

So is a civilian really in command?

Obama meets with General Colin Powell about Afghanistan, who advises, "Don't get pushed by the left to do nothing, or by the right to do everything, or rushed by the media to decide too quickly. Take your time. Whatever you decide will have consequences for the better part of your administration."

Obama has not even finished his first year. General McChrystal, who is the top general in Afghanistan, makes a speech in London with political overtones that shocks even Marine General James L. Jones, the president's tough national security advisor.

Jones tells Gates and Petraeus, "It is a firing offense, but McChrystal won't be fired because we need him." That sounds like some discussions about firing General McClellan that go on in Lincoln's White House.

As it turns out, Lincoln eventually fires McClellan, and Obama eventually fires McChrystal. Maybe civilian presidents do have some power, after all.

Obama tells Bob Woodward, "I had a lot of confidence coming in that the way our system of government works, civilians have to make policy decisions, and then the military carries them out. I am neither intimidated by our military, nor am I thinking that they're somehow trying to undermine my role as commander-in-chief."

Obama is not easily intimidated. Neither is Lincoln, but both of them are sometimes severely limited when it comes to getting the military to do what they want done.

The military is used to seeing presidents come and go. It knows how to work with them, against them, and around them.

Relations with the Supreme Court

It was bound to happen.

Alexis de Tocqueville predicted it his classic *Democracy in America*. He said that there would be clashes between the judiciary, with its unelected justices who serve for life, and the president and Congress, all of whom are elected, and do not serve for life.

Alexis de Tocqueville wrote, "The President may slip without the state suffering, for his duties are limited. Congress may slip without the Union perishing...But if ever the Supreme Court came to be composed of rash or corrupt men, the confederation would be threatened by anarchy or civil war." And, as you will see, this is what happened in 1860.

Is it a fundamental problem if as few as five unelected justices can undo a decision reached by the two other branches of government?

Lincoln

Lincoln thinks it is a problem. In an early draft of his First Inaugural Address, he writes about the "despotism of the few life-officers composing the Court." William Seward convinces Lincoln that his language is too strong. Lincoln deletes those words. But that's what Lincoln really thinks.

Lincoln is not the first president to think this way. Three decades earlier, Andrew Jackson and Chief Justice John Marshall get into bare-knuckle, out-in-the-open fights. The gnarled old hero of the Battle of New Orleans, who still has a bullet or two in him from duels, believes the president of the United States has just as much right to interpret the Constitution as the Court does.

When the Marshall Court rules in favor of the Cherokee Indians, and against the State of Georgia, Jackson supposedly says, "John Marshall has made his decision, now let John Marshall enforce it." Nobody's sure if Jackson actually said those words. But we do know that Jackson never enforced the ruling. Jackson demonstrated that the judicial branch of government is nothing without the executive branch.

That was 1832. Twenty-five years later, the Supreme Court has a new chief justice. His name is Roger B. Taney. By a 7-2 vote, the Taney Court decides the Dred Scott case. The justices rule that the slave Dred Scott and his wife have no right to their freedom.

But the decision goes even further. It rules that neither African American slaves *nor their descendants* have rights as citizens under the Constitution.

That's momentous enough. But the Court is not done yet. It rules that the Missouri Compromise is unconstitutional, and that slavery cannot be legally kept out of the western territories.

The Missouri Compromise is an attempt by Congress to keep slave states and free states together. Slavery has been a problem from the very beginning. But Congress has kept on trying. This particular compromise draws a line across the entire United States at parallel 36° 30'—with slave states below and free states above the line.

That compromise is unconstitutional, the Taney Court rules.

Why? Because it deprives an owner of the right to do whatever he wants to do with his own property. Property rights trump all other rights. Congress has no right to restrict the spread of slavery into the West because this would deprive a slave owner of his property rights.

The decision is momentous. This is the very first time since the Madison Administration that the Supreme Court has ruled that an act of Congress is unconstitutional. The first time was in 1803 in *Marbury v. Madison.* And guess who was chief justice? Andrew Jackson's dear friend, John Marshall.

Whatever the justices may have intended, the consequences of the Dred Scott decision are profound. The compromises that have stitched together a confederation of states are torn apart. Angry quarrels break out. Killings begin.

A political firestorm spreads across the prairies. Abraham Lincoln, who hates slavery, decides to get back into politics. All along Lincoln has expected slavery to die out if it's confined to the South. But if slave owners can bring gangs of slaves to compete with free labor in the fields of the West and down into the gold and silver mines, where will it all end? Lincoln decides to fight. Dred Scott gives us Abraham Lincoln.

And Dred Scott gives us the Republican Party. Meetings are called for everyone to attend who opposes the spread of slavery. Those meetings turn into an organization, and the organization gets to be known as the Republican Party.

Lincoln's partner Billy Herndon joins the organization first. Then Lincoln joins; he criticizes Dred Scott everywhere he gets a chance, and eventually in the famous debates with Stephen Douglas. He devotes a large portion of his famous speech at the Cooper Institute to the subject.

There is many a lesson in Dred Scott. One lesson is that the specifics of a particular decision are not as important as its impact. We can be sure that not one of the seven justices who voted with the majority wanted the Union to be torn apart.

Lincoln could have no way of knowing that he would help overturn Dred Scott. Just eight years after it is decided by the Court, it is overturned by Congress, by the 13th Amendment. Lincoln does everything he can to get the 13th Amendment passed. He calls it "a king's cure" because it closes all the loopholes of the Emancipation Proclamation. There will be no slaves in the West or anywhere else in the US after that Amendment is ratified.

But one more question that Dred Scott raises has not been answered. The Taney Court ruled that African American slaves or their descendants have no rights as citizens. The 14th Amendment, which is passed after Lincoln's death, settles that. It reads, "All persons born or naturalized in the United States, and subject to the jurisdiction thereof, are citizens of the United States and of the State wherein they reside."

Inauguration Day arrives. One of those great ironies of history is about to occur. Roger Taney is the man who will administer the oath of office to Lincoln. Judge Taney! He is sitting on the platform, and has to listen to what the president says about the Supreme Court. Just like another chief justice who is admonished by another president in 2012.

Lincoln has deleted some comments, but not all. He warns against letting the policies of the government be "irrevocably fixed" by the decisions of the Court. If they do, Lincoln says, the people "will have ceased to be their own rulers."

Obama

Like Lincoln, Obama speaks out publicly against the Court. He lectures the justices who are sitting in front of him during his 2012 State of the Union address. Obama takes issue with *Citizens United v. Federal Election Commission*. He believes the Court's decision will change the electoral process, believes if you change how people vote, or who can vote, you change the society. Obama fears that the ruling will open the financial floodgates, and that elections will be drowned in great pools of money.

Ironically, Citizens United comes at a time when individual states are demanding more identification from voters. But this ruling permits super-rich donors to spend as much as they wish on media buys, and do it in secret.

Have the justices thought about the impact of the ruling?

120

In Dred Scott, the court pays more attention to the words of the Constitution than it does to the consequences. Is this an early instance of what today is called *originalism*?

US Supreme Court Associate Justice Antonin Scalia tells how he makes a decision: "What I look for in the Constitution is precisely what I look for in a statute: the original meaning of the text, not what the original craftsman intended."

Isn't this what religious fundamentalists do? Don't they want to know exactly what are the words of St. Paul, what are the words of the *Torah*, the *Koran*?

In the summer of 2012, the nation learns what the Court has decided about the Affordable Care Act. Jeffrey Toobin, legal analyst for CNN, says it should be an easy call. Congress has passed many laws that address health care issues—Medicare, Medicaid, and the like. The courts have always found these laws to be constitutional.

But most observers, liberal and conservative, expect a negative decision.

The decision is announced. It is constitutional. Chief Justice John Roberts has cast the deciding vote.

The right explodes in anger. Chief Justice John Roberts, a George W. Bush appointee, has voted with the 5-4 majority. His Wikipedia listing is vandalized. Beneath his photo, this caption briefly appears: "17th Chief Traitor of the United States."

There is much speculation about just why John Roberts made the decision he did. Even right-wing commentators say that Roberts was thinking about the legitimacy of the Court. And they may be right. An individual can be disrespected and survive. But if the courts are disrespected, anarchy is not far away.

We may never know all that figured into John Robert's decision. My guess is that John Roberts was thinking about *Marbury v. Madison*, and Dred Scott. Whenever five unelected individuals can overturn a law that is duly passed by the elected representatives of the people—the president and Congress—it is risky, it is dangerous.

PUBLIC PERCEPTION

Support from Jewish Americans

The Lincoln and Obama stories regarding public perception could focus on their relationships with the Germans, or with the French, or with the British. Why single out Jewish Americans?

Because something happened to Jewish Americans during the Lincoln administration that dramatically shaped American politics. And, because during the 2012 campaign, the wooing of Jewish support is so visible.

First, what happened in Lincoln's day.

Lincoln

Historian Jonathan D. Sarna has written a new book about a little-known event in Lincoln's time. The book, *When General Grant Expelled the Jews*, is the first one ever written on the subject. [

On December 28, 1862, General Order No. 11 is issued from the headquarters of General U.S. Grant. The order reads:

> *The Jews, as a class having violated every regulation established by the Treasury Department and also department orders, are hereby expelled from the department within 24 hours from the receipt of this order. Post commanders will see that all of this class of people be issued passes and required to leave...*

Notice the words: "Jews, as a class."

Until the 1850s, they are a tiny minority—just 15,000 in the US. But, in the 1850s, over 150,000 emigrate, mainly from Europe.

General Order No. 11 stuns them. Twenty-four hours!

This seems like the brutality they thought they had left behind in Europe. Wasn't America supposed to be "the land of the free and the home of the brave" that Francis Scott Key wrote back in 1814, and Americans had been singing ever since? Maybe they had made a mistake. Maybe America is just like the places they had fled.

The order gets a lot of attention. Newspapers devote many columns to it. It is debated on the floor of Congress.

The American Jewish community has never been in the political spotlight like this before.

They mobilize. Delegations set off to Washington, hoping to see President Lincoln. They are successful. Lincoln immediately revokes the order of a general he thinks a lot of. Lincoln praises the efforts of the 6,000 to 8,000 Jewish Americans who are fighting for the Union. He says he does not like to hear "an entire class or nationality condemned on account of the few sinners."

These immigrants are learning that in America their voice can be heard all the way to the White House. They get positive reinforcement instead of persecution for claiming their rights as citizens.

But something even more significant happens. General Grant is remorseful, and later apologizes publicly. Grant does a 180-degree turn. When he becomes president six years later, he sets out to atone for General Order No. 11, one that his wife Julia refers to as "that obnoxious order."

Grant appoints more Jews to public office than any of his predecessors, and aids persecuted Jews in Russia and Romania.

But there's more. Grant does not lend his support to repeated attempts to pass a religious amendment declaring that the United States "is a Christian nation."

If that amendment had become a part of the Constitution, Jews and members of other religions would not be on an equal footing with Christians. The distinction is profound, because there is a difference between religious *toleration* and religious *freedom*.

Thanks to what happened as a result of Grant's order—the most notorious anti-Jewish order by a government official in American history—a larger definition is given to the words "we the people."

Obama

In the 2008 race, Obama gets 78 percent of the Jewish vote. American Jews have supported liberal causes too long to abandon the first black president. Jews passionately supported the Civil Rights Movement. Along with other groups, they donated, they marched, they were arrested and beaten. Two Jewish civil rights workers—Andrew Goodwin and Michael Schwerner—were murdered with James Chaney, their black friend, in Philadelphia, Mississippi.

Obama's triumph is viewed as a victory for the Civil Rights Movement. Besides, the Obama story is an outsider story. And Jewish Americans understand what it's like to be outsiders.

One of Obama's first big donors is Penny Pritzker, a noted philanthropist associated with the Hyatt hotel fortune. With her support and contacts, Obama raises $6 million for his primary run for the US Senate. He wins the primary, and crushes Republican

Alan Keyes in the general election. Pritzker will eventually head Obama's finance committee, which under Pritzker's leadership, raises record-breaking amounts of contributions during the presidential primaries.

The 2012 Obama re-election site boasts a special "Jewish Americans for Obama" page. In July 2012, President Obama imposes new sanctions on Iran, and renews his pledge of friendship to Israel. Obama signs into law the US-Israel Enhanced Security Cooperation Act of 2012, which re-affirms the nation's commitment to the State of Israel and the US-Israel relationship. Meanwhile, Governor Romney makes a highly visible trip to Israel. A senior Romney advisor tells a journalist that the whole trip was worth doing just to get a photograph of Romney at the Wailing Wall.

In a 2012 American Jewish Committee survey, 61 percent say they support President Obama whereas 28 percent support Republican candidate Mitt Romney. Breaking the numbers out, Obama has the support of 67 percent of Jewish women, and 55 percent of Jewish men. Romney has the support of 34 percent of Jewish men and 22 percent of women. Among Jewish Americans, polls show Obama receiving high marks from the Jewish community for his support of gay rights, women's issues, and civil rights. Obama gets 63 percent of the Jewish vote in 2012.

Admired and Loved In Foreign Countries

Lincoln

Lincoln is a much-loved president abroad, and his reputation is wearing well.

Not by wealthy aristocrats. Not at the beginning, anyway. But among the mill workers, it's another story. The mill workers in Manchester hold rallies for the Union cause. They're out of work, tens of thousands of them, and many are starving. The mills are closed. Nine out of ten inhabitants in the region work in the mills, and there's no cotton. It's been cut off by the Northern blockade of Southern ports. Nevertheless the workers are supporting Lincoln, and the North, and the abolition of slavery, and the cause of freedom.

A bronze statue of Lincoln stands today in downtown Manchester, England On the base is this inscription:

ABRAHAM LINCOLN

Born 12 February 1809
Assassinated 15 April,1865
President of the USA
1861-1865
American civil war
15 April,1861-9 April,1865
Lancashire cotton famine
1861-1865
The statue (above) commemorates the support that the working people of Manchester gave in the fight for the abolition of slavery during the American civil war.

The Emancipation Proclamation has done it. When Lincoln issues it, the Civil War acquires a different meaning, another narrative. No longer is it a war between sections of the country. It is a moral issue—slavery versus freedom. Any hopes that the political leaders of Europe have of recognizing and supporting the Confederacy are gone.

Admiration of Lincoln abroad has never diminished. There are multiple statues of Lincoln in Mexico, and if you go to London, you will see only one statue of an American in Parliament Square—Lincoln's.

Obama

A rapturous crowd of 200,000 is waiting in Berlin. Obama is consciously repeating history in the city where JFK gave his speech in 1963, and Ronald Reagan gave his in 1987. Berliners love him. He is signaling a change in foreign policy. No more go-it-alone, Obama says. "The greatest danger of all is allowing new walls to divide us from one another."

He is a celebrity abroad, as popular as a rock star. All the polls show that foreigners begin to view America more favorably as soon as Obama is elected. They can't understand the hatred toward him from some quarters in America.

Here are some international headlines and editorials that announce Obama's victory:

Dominic Mahlangu and Jackie May write in *The Times* (Johannesburg): "There has never been any doubt that if the rest of the world had been eligible to vote in the US presidential election, Obama's victory would have been virtually absolute."

The Telegraph, Calcutta:

"Forty-five years after Martin Luther King had a dream, America wakes up to a new dawn."

The Globe and Mail of Toronto, Canada:

"Obama overcomes. Yes he can! Massive turnout delivers the most votes ever cast for a US presidential candidate."

A newspaper in Tel Aviv carries this headline:
"The Hope of America"

PRESIDENTIAL SETBACKS AND ACHIEVEMENTS

Early Issues

Both overestimate the power of logic and facts in winning over opponents. Lincoln believes slave-owners care more about the Union than they do about their economic interests. Obama believes politicians care more about the good of the nation than they do about being re-elected.

Lincoln

He clings to the belief that most Southerners love the Union more than they do, that they will not secede. He is wrong, of course.

It is January 1861, in the middle of what historians call "the great secession winter." Lincoln is still in Springfield, and it is nerve-wracking. He won't take office until March. Inaugurations occur in March in the 1860s. South Carolina, Mississippi, Florida, Georgia and Alabama have already voted to secede. Hapless James Buchanan sits in the White House, paralyzed.

A letter arrives in Springfield from a Republican Congressman named James T. Hale urging Lincoln to help revive the Missouri Compromise.

Hale knows that would mean slave states all the way to the Pacific, but it just might save the Union. On today's map, Oklahoma, New Mexico, Arizona, and Southern California are below the line—so slavery would be allowed there if the change is made.

Lincoln can back down on one big issue, and maybe avoid a civil war.

Lincoln knows what is at stake. The Republican Party has been founded on the principle that slavery will never ever be allowed to expand into the West.

So, what to do?

Here is what Lincoln writes to Hale:

> *We have just carried an election on principles fairly stated to the people. Now we are told in advance, the government shall be broken up, unless we surrender to those we have beaten, before we take the offices...If we surrender, it is the end of us, and of the government. They*

will repeat the experiment upon us ad libitum...*There is, in my judgment, but one compromise which would really settle the slavery question, and that would be a prohibition against acquiring any more territory.*

By temperament and by habit Lincoln seeks compromise. For years, as a lawyer, he has advised his clients to compromise. And in politics Lincoln has made compromises again and again. He knows that the United States itself is a compromise between large states and small, between capital and labor, rich and poor.

Lincoln knows all that. But this is a deal-breaker. The demands are too great. The very existence of the Republican Party, and the government, is what is on the table.

If Republicans yield on this, there is no further reason to have a party.

Lincoln is finally disabused of the idea that the secessionists are bargaining in good faith. He recognizes that the secessionists love their region and their peculiar institution more than they do the Union. He is convinced that the secessionists will be back with more demands if they win this round.

Lincoln tells a Springfield visitor, "By no act or complicity of mine shall the Republican Party become a mere sucked egg, all shell and no principle to it."

Lincoln is learning, but there are more lessons ahead.

The Fort Sumter crisis arises. Lincoln bypasses his Secretary of the Navy. As a result, the *USS Powhatan* gets conflicting orders. One set of orders sends it to Fort Pickens in Florida; the other sends it to Fort Sumter in the harbor of Charleston, S.C. to provide provisions for besieged Union troops stationed there. It's a complicated story of micromanaging. Welles later writes,

"Never from that day, to the close of his life, was there any interference with the administration of the Navy Department, nor was any step taken without first consulting me."

Lincoln pushes General Irvin McDowell to fight a battle too soon. The general warns Lincoln that his troops are green. Lincoln replies that the rebels are green, too. He thinks a show of force will make the rebels back down. George Washington did that successfully in the Whiskey Rebellion. Go ahead and fight, Lincoln orders.

And fight they do, at Bull Run. It is a rout of Union forces. The enemy chases them almost all the way back to Washington. Months will pass before there is a major Union victory.

Disaster would not be too harsh a word for Lincoln's first three years in the presidency. Congress is in rebellion. The mid-term election is a gigantic setback. Congress has created the Joint Committee on the Conduct of the War, and it is poking its nose into everything. Early in 1864, Lincoln tells his cabinet that he does not expect to be re-elected in November.

But Lincoln is learning. Horace Greeley writes: "He was open to all impressions and influences, and gladly profited by the teachings of events and circumstances, no matter how adverse or unwelcome."

Obama

He promises to close Guantanamo within a year. He tries hard to keep his promise, but is blocked in Congress. He promises to get out of Iraq on a timetable. He keeps that promise.

Obama believes he can work with his foes. He reaches across the aisle. His foes say he doesn't reach far enough. He makes concessions. They ask for more.

MSNBC's Rachel Maddow says on the air, "Obama, they're just not into you." Obama says, I know people think I'm naive for believing I can work with Republicans, but I'm going to keep trying. All the while, Republican Senator Mitch McConnell from Kentucky says that Republican's number one goal is making sure Obama is a one-term President.

Obama's opponents decide that there's no cost involved if they oppose him, but there's the Devil to pay if they work with him, or even pose with him for a photo. They get emails warning them that if they go along with Obama's agenda, they can forget about re-election

It's understandable why Obama clings to the bipartisan dream so long. He wants to keep his promise. He wants to turn his campaign slogan into a reality. He wants to bring people together. He has told millions that they can expect something different from him, not just business-as-usual Washington.

He decides to invite Republicans and Democrats over to the White House for a kind of town meeting on health care. It will be on TV—CSPAN from start to finish. The big networks will pick up the juiciest parts. House members sit on the right, senators on the left. Obama sits in the center. John and Mitch McConnell are to his left. Nancy Pelosi and Harry Reid to his right.

Obama displays his command of facts, his facile mind. But it makes little impact. The Republicans stare at him. He tries to draw in Mitch McConnell. He refers to him by name. McConnell just looks at him. He tries to engage John McCain. There's a testy exchange.

How many American voters who watch change their minds? It's hard to say.

One thing is sure. Nothing changes in Congress. If anything, the climate has worsened. The only positive outcome is Harry Reid and Nancy Pelosi patch up their differences. The Republicans and Democrats may not work together, but Democrats in both Houses will.

Obama arrives at the conclusion that Lincoln did—that he can't be the one who makes all the concessions. He says, "Bipartisanship can't be that I agree to all the things that they believe in or want, and they agree to none of the things I believe in and want."

His chief political advisor David Axelrod says: "I think there are people who want to be helpful who want to do the right thing. I think they're terribly frightened right now. They're frightened by their own leadership, and they're frightened by the sort of rage within their own party. So the reasonable people are running for the hills."

Another top Obama advisor says the eye-opener took place when they realized during negotiations over raising the debt ceiling that there were people who were willing to let the nation go over the cliff if they didn't get their way.

A White House correspondent says, "He's tried to be a nice guy. Now he's picking a fight because the situation demands it, and he has no choice but a Harry Truman strategy"

Creating "Teams of Rivals"

Doris Kearns Goodwin writes a best-seller about Lincoln's cabinet, and gives it the title *Team of Rivals*. When you hear the word "team," you think of players working for a common goal. The Yankees and the Red Sox, the Steelers and the Saints, the Heat and the Lakers winning games, trophies, championships.

But there is rivalry on the best of teams.

For example, there is rivalry to make the team. Few can be chosen. A coach must think about getting all the skills needed, all the positions covered. Presidents do that. They make sure that states and regions and important constituencies are represented on the team. Lincoln chooses conservatives and radicals, Whigs and Democrats, Easterners and Westerners.

Lincoln can't have two people from the same state, no matter how talented they might be. He has to spread the honors around. He even considers asking his old friend Alexander Stephens of Georgia to be a cabinet member. He wants the South to be represented. But Stephens has other plans. He becomes vice president of the Confederacy instead.

Obama chooses women and ethnic minorities from various regions. He makes three offers to Republicans, and gets two. Secretary of Transportation Ray LaHood and Secretary of Defense Robert Gates.

It's all about gaining political support. Remember what Lincoln believes about public opinion. It is everything. Nothing can succeed without it.

There's also rivalry over positions. A player might really want to be a quarterback, but settle for defensive back. The secretary of interior might really want to be secretary of state, the postmaster general might really want treasury. But they settle for what they can get, just to be on the team.

There's rivalry between coach and players, too. Players often think they know more than the coach. That certainly is true of Lincoln's cabinet. At least initially. By the end, even Seward is admitting that he could never do what Lincoln has done.

We don't yet know much about how Obama's cabinet members feel about each other, or their feelings about the president. We will when they publish their memoirs. In coming years, we doubtless will read accounts similar to the ones that members of Lincoln's cabinet wrote.

There's rivalry over who gets to stay, and who must go. Coaches have to make decisions about whether to get rid of a talented but disruptive player, hold on to a player who's in a slump, choose a veteran instead of a gifted rookie. Presidents do that, too.

Two examples. Lincoln decides to let his first Secretary of Defense Simon Cameron go. He's inept, and Lincoln becomes convinced he's also corrupt. But Cameron has strong support in the important state of Pennsylvania, so he can't fire him outright. Lincoln offers him an ambassadorship, and sends him off to Russia. He tells a friend to warn the hostesses of St. Petersburg to hide their best silverware.

Lincoln has to decide about Salmon Chase as well. Chase has considerable influence, and he is one of the few individuals who has the requisite knowledge to run the Department of Treasury. But Chase is insubordinate and disloyal. His desire to be president gets in his way, and Lincoln is forced to let him go.

Obama has not fired any cabinet officer, but he has nudged out a few top advisors.

There's also rivalry between players who want to be the star, to be the one with the picture in the paper. In a cabinet, even if the rivalry is not personal, there is a constant struggle among the departments they represent plus debates over ideas and strategy. There was never a time when there was not some clash of ideas or personalities in Lincoln's cabinet.

As for Obama, there is more than one team that he has to think about. There's Obama's cabinet, of course, which parallels Lincoln's, but there are other high-level teams Obama must work with on defense, the economy, plus his political team.

Bob Woodward gives a vivid account of the behind-the-scene debates over what to do about Afghanistan in *Obama's Wars*. He describes long, intense debates among Biden and the NSA advisor James Jones, Secretary of State Hillary Clinton, Secretary of Defense Robert Gates and the political advisors and the Chairman of the Joint Chiefs of Staff Michael Mullen.

And Afghanistan is just one issue the president must deal with. Later in the day the president will meet with another team, another cast of characters. This time it might be about the economy. And this debate could be as intense as the one he just left.

This kind of rivalry is built into the office. For as long as anyone can remember, there has been rivalry between the Army and the Navy, the State Department and the Defense Department, between the president and members of his cabinet. They fight over funding, over assignments, over offices, over access to the president.

It is not a question of patriotism. Everyone in the cabinet and the various teams want Team America to win. The rivalry is over what strategy to follow, how it will get funded, which people to use, and who gets credit for the win or blame for the loss.

Lincoln

Lincoln's Treasury Secretary Chase complains, "There is no administration properly speaking...We have as little to do with it [the war] as if we were heads of factories supplying shoes and clothing."

Lincoln's cabinet meetings often lack systematic reporting, and they are sometimes poorly attended. Tension is always just beneath the surface, and occasionally boils up.

But Lincoln does listen to his cabinet, even if he keeps his own counsel, makes up his own mind. He will ask them to write position papers. He tries out ideas on the cabinet. Debates with them. Invites them to play devil's advocate. He delays announcing the Emancipation Proclamation on their advice. In one instance, Lincoln abandons a plan he deeply cares about—*compensated emancipation*. He thinks it will end the war if the government purchases slaves from their owners, and then frees them. He pushes the idea in Congress, with his cabinet, runs the numbers. He gets nowhere. Finally he says in despair, "You are all against me."

Lincoln has very little contact with his two vice presidents, Hannibal Hamlin and Andrew Johnson. He treats them almost as non-entities. Lincoln prefers to work one-on-one with individual members of the cabinet, often with Stanton and Seward and with his military advisors. As he approaches the end of his first term, Lincoln spends more time with politicians, journalists, and political advisors.

Obama

Critics complain that Obama's cabinet is not very Lincolnesque, but they seem not to know how Lincoln's cabinet really operated. This is often the case with imagined history. We want the greats of the past to behave in the way we imagine they should have behaved.

Obama's team does not have officers who campaign secretly against the president, as Salmon Chase did. But it is Lincolnesque in some respects. Both cabinets have very prominent political figures, as well as obscure, almost anonymous ones.

Obama spends the most time with Secretary of State Clinton and Vice President Biden—his rivals for the presidency—with Treasury Secretary Timothy Geithner, and with the Secretary of Defense and his national security advisors. And as his re-election campaign heats up, just as Lincoln did, Obama spends increasing amounts of time with his political team.

Symbols

Symbols inspire, create moods, evoke memories, arouse to action, and tell stories without words. That is what a cross on a church spire, a Purple Heart, a prayer vigil are intended to do.

Great leaders in every field understand the power of symbols, and use them. It is Lincoln finishing the Capitol dome. It is Obama inviting special guests to sit on the front row of the balcony with the First Lady during the State of the Union Address. The guests say nothing, but their presence does.

Lincoln

They ask Lincoln if he wants to finish the dome of the Capitol. It's still a squatty, half-finished project with scaffolding up the sides of the building. The funds required to complete it are needed for the war. Finish the dome later, some say. It's just for show anyway. What else is a big dome good for?

"Finish it," Lincoln says. He knows it is for show. It shows he intends to see this thing through. It shows he plans to win. It shows the Union will endure.

Obama

He launches his campaign from the steps of the Old State Capitol in Springfield, thereby creating an association with Lincoln. He poses with Lilly Ledbetter, who is a symbol of pay disparity, when he signs into law an act that will expand women's rights.

He invokes the memory of his mother Ann Dunham—who died of uterine and ovarian cancer in 1995—when he signs the Affordable Care Act. "Today I'm signing this reform bill into law on behalf of my mother, who argued with insurance companies even as she battled cancer in her final days."

Appealing to the "Better Angels" of Our Nature

Throughout history, leaders have come to power by exploiting hatred and fear. They stir up prejudices against Jews, Catholics, Protestants, Muslims, Christians, Armenians, Germans, Arabs, Indians, Japanese, Koreans, Chinese. It is the story of pogroms and lynchings, purges and racial cleansings, books like *Mein Kampf* and the *Protocols of the Elders of Zion.*

> It is an impulse as old as history—hating the stranger, the foreigner, the outsider. The targets and situations change, but the motivations are similar.

And then there are leaders who appeal to our generosity, our kindness, our sense of duty and justice, to all the good things we are capable of being.

In Lincoln's time, the Know-Nothings fed on what is worst in us— fear, and bigotry, and hatred.

Today immigrants are the target. Just listen to haters on talk radio, read their emails, visit their websites. Ask yourself if they appeal to what is best in anybody.

There is not a hint of this in President Lincoln or President Obama. Go over their presidential speeches and letters with a magnifying glass and you will not find it.

Obama is accused of stirring up class hatred because he believes profitable corporations and the very rich should bear a larger tax burden than they now do.

To call this "class hatred" is as bogus as saying Lincoln stirred up class hatred against slave owners when he denounced the institution of slavery.

In an essay that President Obama contributes to *The Atlantic*, he describes the famous Lincoln photograph that Alexander Gardner took shortly before the President's death (pictured on the back of this book): "Three years before he entered Gardner's studio, Lincoln termed the United States...'the last best hope of earth.' Considering that our fragile Union was not one hundred years old and stood a good chance of dissolving, it was an improbable thing to say...He saw us not only as we were, but as we might be. And he calls on us through the ages to commit ourselves to the unfinished work he so nobly advanced—the work of perfecting our Union."

VI.
THE WORLD: THEN AND NOW

There is a tide in the affairs of men. Which, taken at the flood, leads on to fortune; Omitted, all the voyage of their life is bound in shallows and in miseries. On such a full sea are we now afloat, and we must take the current when it serves, or lose our ventures.

– Shakespeare, *Julius Caesar*

THE WORLD: THEN AND NOW

Some parallels in history are sociological. Similar social settings produce similar types of individuals. Bureaucracies create individuals who behave in predictable ways, whether the bureaucracy is the Department of Defense, a major university, or a large corporation.

The American presidency creates behavior that's predictable too.

What presidents can do, and not do, and how long they can do it, is set by the job. Presidents are defined by the problems that get handed to them, the circumstances they have to deal with. Lincoln understands this. He says, "I freely confess, I have not controlled events. Events have controlled me."

Theodore Roosevelt states: "If there is not the war, you don't get the great general; if there is not a great occasion, you don't get a great statesman; if Lincoln had lived in a time of peace, no one would have known his name."

Rahm Emanuel, Obama's chief of staff, points toward the Oval Office: "You know what ends up down in that office? Bad and worse. Those are your choices. And the time frame they're on is immediate and crisis. That's the axis."

Here is the world that Lincoln and Obama come to, and produces what ends up on their desks.

Economic Panics: Then...And Now

A great economic collapse of global proportions occurs just prior to Lincoln's presidency—the Panic of 1857.

A great economic collapse of global proportions occurs in 2007—the beginning of the Great Recession—just prior to the Obama presidency.

There had been panics and bank failures in the United States before 1857. But this one is global. Great Britain, in particular, is shaken, and has to manipulate its currency.

A historian describes the months leading up to the panic: "Since the years immediately preceding the Panic of 1857 were prosperous, many banks, merchants and farmers had seized the opportunity to take risks with their investments."

In the 1850s, railroads look very attractive to investors. Railroads are the new high tech. Investors loan railroads huge sums. Then things take a downward turn. Grain prices fall. Farmers can't pay mortgages. Businesses fail. Banks foreclose on property. A big insurance company goes under. It's a tipping point. Railroads can't repay their loans. There are layoffs. The economy struggles. The recovery is slow.

It's 2007. The crash occurs during the closing days of the George W. Bush Administration. It is so severe it's called a depression, not just a recession, by Nobel laureate economist Paul Krugman.

Both presidents—Lincoln and Obama—inherit a political and economic mess. By the time Lincoln gets into office, federal armories and forts and depots and vast amounts of ammunition have fallen into rebel hands. One of the big questions Lincoln faces as soon as he becomes president is whether to re-take the forts. Doing that is deemed too hostile by his advisors. He settles on trying to hold the two big forts that are left—Sumter and Pickens. He will eventually lose Fort Sumter.

Obama inherits two wars and a collapsing economy. During the George W. Bush years, the booming real estate market has cloaked the disappearance of entire industries. Some industries have been gone so long when Obama takes office that the factories and plants and mills are shuttered or turned into lofts. Only ghosts remain of what once fueled the economy: garment making, shipyards, paper mills, big steel mills, TV manufacturing, cotton mills. Most are gone overseas. Even many high-tech jobs are leaving.

When Obama mentions any of this, his foes say it is finger-pointing. But this is what the American economic landscape is like in the twenty-first century, regardless of who is president.

Obama is like Lincoln, who inherits just two forts. Obama is blamed for not reviving the economy to its former vigor. Obama will look for something to hold on to, some sector of the economy to revive. But much of what used to be at the core of the economy is gone.

Political Parties They Are a' Changin'

Then...

During the 1840s and 1850s, the major political parties re-invent themselves. The Federalist Party, which once boasted big names like Alexander Hamilton and John Adams, has disappeared. Most Federalists have moved into the Whig Party, which for a while is a national power, with names like John Tyler and Henry Clay. But now the Whigs are weak and dying, too.

Meanwhile the Democrats are moving hard right. They will soon split over slavery and states' rights. The Republican Party is emerging.

They are a mixed bag, these Republicans—former Whigs, and anti-slavery Democrats, abolitionists and members of smaller parties, like the Free-Soilers, and, yes, some Know-Nothings. One reason they settle on the name Republican is its association with Thomas Jefferson, especially his words in the Declaration of Independence: "All men are created equal." Lincoln quotes Thomas Jefferson repeatedly.

As for the Democrats, the party still bears the image of Andrew Jackson. Andrew Jackson to Democrats then is what Ronald Reagan is to Republicans today.

What did Democrats believe then? Pretty much what Republicans believe today.

Here's how the *Democratic Review* summarizes their creed: "As little government as possible; that little emanating from and controlled by the people..."

And what did the Whigs, who evolve into Republicans, believe then? Pretty much what Democrats believe today.

Horace Greeley, of the *New York Tribune,* writes that Whigs do not regard government "with disgust and aversion...Our philosophy regards a Government with hope and confidence, as an agency of the community through which vast and beneficent ends may be accomplished."

Lincoln, remember, is a Whig. Lincoln believes that the object of government is "to do for the people whatever needs to be done, but which they cannot by individual effort, do at all, or do so well, for themselves."

And now...

Since the latter part of the twentieth century, the Republican Party has been re-inventing itself, purging itself of liberal, left-leaning elements. It is light years from the Republican Party of Lincoln, Theodore Roosevelt, or Dwight Eisenhower.

Political scientists who study the voting record of Republicans in Congress over the past few decades find that Republicans have moved much farther to the right than Democrats have moved to the left.

Obama is giving a speech about this change at the University of Vermont. He says, "The first Republican president, President Lincoln, couldn't win the nomination for the Republican primary right now."

He invokes the names of other Republican presidents. "It was a Republican, Teddy Roosevelt, who called for a progressive income tax." Today's Republicans are clamoring for a flat tax.

"It was Dwight Eisenhower [a Republican] who built the Interstate highway system."

Obama gets personal, "It was with the help of Republicans that FDR was able to give millions of returning heroes, including my grandfather, the chance to go to college through the GI Bill."

At the time Dwight Eisenhower leaves office, there are liberals, moderates, and conservatives in the Republican Party. Getting rid of the liberals and moderates begins in earnest after Goldwater is nominated. The purge continues during the Reagan years, and throughout the presidency of George W. Bush.

There are virtually no liberals who call themselves liberals left in today's Republican Party. To be fair, there are Republicans who are liberal on social issues, such as gay rights.

General Colin Powell is a Republican. In recent years Powell has been prominently mentioned as a presidential or a vice-presidential possibility. Powell tells a friend he has major reservations about "the intolerant tone that seems to be overtaking the Republican Party." Powell says he doesn't like "the hate-soaked rallies." He ends up endorsing Obama in 2008.

In Eisenhower's day, Republican strength is in the North and West. It barely has a presence in the South.

Then comes LBJ. As long as Johnson is a senator from Texas, he is a staunch segregationist. Johnson says he has an obligation, as a representative of Texans, to vote the way his constituents believe. But when LBJ becomes president, he pivots, saying he needs to do what is best for the nation, even if that's not what Texans want.

He pushes the Civil Rights Act, manages to get it through Congress, and signs it into law in 1964. When a photograph is taken at the signing ceremony, MLK is standing right behind him.

Johnson predicts that Democrats will lose the South for a generation. He is wrong. It's not been one generation. It's been two generations, going on three.

The Deep South is now as solid red as it once was solid blue. More and more, Republicans think and talk Southern.

Here's a joke about Republicans:

"Did you hear that African-American Republicans are holding a convention this year?"
"No. Where are they gonna' hold it?"
"In a phone booth."

It's an old joke. There aren't that many phone booths left. But you get the point.

Obama gets 95 percent of the black vote in 2008 and 93 percent in 2012. Identity politics certainly plays a role in that whopping percentage.

Some voters will always let their identification with a particular ethnic group or religion determine their decisions in the voting booth. A lot of American Catholics voted for Kennedy because he was a Catholic, and Romney will get a high proportion of the Mormon vote.

But identity politics was not as big a factor as some people imagine in the 2008 election. It is a small percentage, no matter who you ask or how you qualify the question: According to a 2004 study 13.7% of blacks identified as "conservative" or "extremely conservative" with another 14.4% identifying as slightly conservative. However the same study indicated less than 10% identified as Republican or Republican-leaning in any fashion.

Likewise, a recent Pew Research Center survey showed that 19% of blacks identify as Religious Right. In 2012, the Pew Research Center indicated only 4% of blacks identify as Republican.

Blacks vote for Democrats in large numbers, even when the candidate is white.

That's a huge change from what it was for decades. For decades after the Civil War, when blacks were allowed to vote, they voted Republican. They hung pictures of Lincoln on their walls. But in the mid-twentieth century, a change occurs. The pictures on the walls are of JFK and MLK. Blacks know how to pivot, too.

Nothing could stir up more passion among Republicans in Lincoln's day than slavery. Today, the big passion-arousers are abortion, contraception, gay marriage, immigration, taxation, government regulation, and Obamacare—the Republican's preferred name for the Affordable Care Act.

The Republican Party has internal tensions that could split it apart. It is wrestling with how to get the Latino vote, but this is a problem because of its opposition to amnesty of undocumented immigrants and to the DREAM Act, which would give some young Latinos a path to citizenship.

Meanwhile the Democrats have made it more difficult for Republicans to woo Latinos. The Obama administration has halted the deportation of young people who were brought here illegally as children. Obama used existing executive authority—"prosecutorial discretion"—to stop deporting young, law-abiding immigrants. The result: 800,000 young people can finish school and find work without fear of deportation.

Pulitzer Prize-winning author Steve Coll writes: "The decision is no 'Emancipation Proclamation,' but it has some of that document's transformational quality: there are a few moments when a President with a single act, can immediately uplift and legitimatize the lives of so many."

There are parallels. The Emancipation Proclamation is an executive order. It is temporary. It is controversial. The decision to halt deportation of young Latinos is by executive order, too. And it is temporary. It is controversial.

In point of fact, Obama pushed hard to get the DREAM Act passed in 2010, but Republicans were able to block it in the Senate.

The GOP also must find a way to keep rich, traditional Republicans and populist Tea Party types under the same tent.

What to do with the Libertarians, who view establishment Republicans with distrust? The Libertarians want the smallest government possible. If orthodox Libertarians have their way, everything that's not explicitly mandated in the Constitution will be phased out. That means Social Security and Medicare, plus foreign aid to friendly nations, which means real trouble at the ballot box.

As for the Democrats, it still has elements of the coalition that FDR created—labor, moderates, progressives, liberals, minorities, Catholics. Everything except the aforementioned Southerners.

There's a strong anti-war element in the Democratic Party, which vehemently opposed the Iraq War, and is not one bit happy about the Afghanistan War. But the alternative is worse, in their opinion, so virtually all have remained Democrats.

The Catholics are another part of the FDR coalition, but there are strains between Catholic liberals, who favor a woman's right to choose, and the Catholic bishops. The bishops are decidedly anti-choice, and oppose government-mandated health care policies because of birth control coverage.

It feels like the 1860s again. Party-feeling is high, divisions between right and left are sharp, attacks on the president are venomous, and Congress is paralyzed.

States' Rights

Then...

Three decades before the Civil War, South Carolina threatens to secede. Its state militia begins to drill. Andrew Jackson sends a message down to South Carolina. He says they can talk as much as they want to, but if they do more than talk, he will lead the Army into the state with a rope in his hand to hang traitors. He has former vice president and now Senator John Calhoun in mind as a prime candidate. South Carolina backs down, but secessionist sentiment continues to fester. Jackson later reportedly says the biggest regret of his life is not hanging John Calhoun.

The secessionists in Jackson's and Lincoln's day make much of the 10th Amendment, which reads: "The powers not delegated to the United States by the Constitution, nor prohibited by it to the States, are reserved to the States respectively, or to the people."

Lincoln knows the 10th Amendment has been taken almost verbatim from the old Articles of Confederation. He also knows the Articles of Confederation was a failure. It gave the federal government too little power, and the states too much power. That first version of the United States lasted just eight years. When James Madison introduces the 10th Amendment, he admits it is "superfluous" and "unnecessary." But some states demand it.

The Civil War weakens the power of individual states, and enhances federal power.

Before Lincoln's administration, the United States is referred to in the plural. The United States "are." After Lincoln, the United States begins to be referred to in the singular. The United States "is." Lincoln turns the United States into a nation.

When the Civil War begins, two confederacies face one another. People at the time use the word "confederacy" when they refer to the Union. By the end of the war, a confederacy in the South is fighting a *nation* in the North.

Lincoln understands that a loose arrangement of little sovereign republics is too weak to survive. When he gives his inaugural address in 1861, Lincoln does not use the word "nation" a single time. Two years later, at Gettysburg, Lincoln refers to the United States five times in two minutes as a "nation."

The United States becomes "one nation, under God, indivisible."

And now...

There are calls for more states' rights, less federal government. Within a week after Obama's re-election, hundreds of thousands of Americans in all fifty states sign petitions to secede from the United States. Tenth-Amendment politicians talk like the Civil War never happened.

There is a backlash to the secession petitioners. Strip the petition signers of their citizenship rights, some say, or require them all to read *Gone with the Wind.*

Obama, in his inaugural address, says bigger or smaller is not the question. "The question we ask today is not whether our government is too big or too small, but whether it works."

In early 2012 Wisconsin Governor Scott Walker is a guest on *Face the Nation.* He tells the host he believes health care should be given back to the states. It's no business of the federal government.

Walker is not alone. It's become a litany. The states are good. The federal government is bad. But that does not stop Governor Walker just a few months later in July of 2012 from requesting federal aid for the drought that has hit his state. Walker does not see any hypocrisy in the request.

The Obama administration has a fight with several states over immigration policy. Arizona leads the way with its "papers please" law, but Georgia and Alabama are not far behind. Georgia passes an immigration law so strict that migrant workers flee. Millions of dollars of crops rot in the fields. Alabama passes a law that requires public schools to check the legal status of students. Enrollment of Latino children plummets.

Presently, voting requirements vary from state to state. Requirements should be standardized for national elections. It doesn't matter to residents of Ohio who gets to vote for governor or mayor or dog catcher in Mississippi. But who Mississippi sends to Congress, or how they vote for president does matter. Of course, the only way this change can happen is by a Supreme Court decision or a Constitutional Amendment.

Turmoil in the Churches

Then...

During the mid-1800s religious denominations split over slavery. Baptists in the South, who mainly accept slavery, split away from Baptists in the North. They call themselves the Southern Baptist Convention. They still do. The Southern Baptist Convention today is the largest Protestant denomination in America. The Methodists and Presbyterians split over slavery too, but after the war they get back together.

The split is mainly geographical, since most of the slaves are concentrated in the South. But there are a few anti-slavery preachers in the South, and some pro-slavery preachers in the North.

The Catholic Church does not split geographically. In the South, where Catholics are a small minority, Catholics mainly accommodate to the dominant view. The Catholic Church does not officially condemn slavery, and is generally unfriendly toward abolitionists. Irish Catholic immigrants are especially hostile toward abolitionists because they fear that an influx of freed slaves into the north will take away their jobs.

And now...

There are quarrels among liberals and conservatives and ultra-conservatives in churches, temples, synagogues, and mosques. Denominations are splintering. One small town I visit in Nebraska has Lutheran churches affiliated with three different synods, and a fourth one is meeting in temporary quarters because the other three are too liberal. The Episcopal Church is split over the issue of gay bishops. American Catholic women have issues with a hierarchy dominated by single men.

These religious quarrels spill over into politics, often determining which party religious individuals choose, and the candidates they vote for. Some churches print ratings of candidates on key issues, somewhat like horse-racing tip-sheets, for members to take with them when they vote.

A Contentious Congress

Then...

May 22, 1856, Washington, D.C.: Massachusetts Senator Charles Sumner, an outspoken foe of slavery, is attacked by South Carolina Congressman Preston Brooks while seated at his desk in Congress. Sumner almost dies. Congressman Brooks becomes a hero. Replicas of the metal-tipped cane that Brooks uses in the attack become sought-after souvenirs.

And now...

January 24, 2011, Washington, D.C: President Obama is in the middle of the State of the Union address. He says something that Republican Congressman Joe Wilson from South Carolina doesn't agree with. Wilson shouts out, "You lie." Wilson's fundraising surges. He becomes a popular speaker at Tea Party events. Bumper stickers and tee shirts with the words "You Lie" are on sale.

The Media Covers Parallel Universes

Then... And now...

"Consider the source" is what Americans sometimes say when they hear a rumor.

Look at newspaper comments about the Gettysburg Address—by their source.

The *Chicago Times*: "The cheeks of every American must tingle with shame as he reads the silly, flat and dishwatery utterances."

The *Chicago Times* is an anti-Lincoln paper. It finds fault with virtually everything Lincoln does.

Another newspaper in Chicago—the *Tribune*—is pro-Lincoln. This is the *Tribune's* account: "The dedicatory remarks by President Lincoln will live among the annals of man."

The *Springfield* (Massachusetts) *Republican* is pro-Lincoln. It prints this report: "Surprisingly fine as Mr. Everett's oration was in the Gettysburg consecration, the rhetorical honors of the occasion were won by President Lincoln. His little speech is a perfect gem; deep in feeling, compact in thought and expression, and tasteful and elegant in every word and comma."

The *Harrisburg (Pennsylvania) Patriot and Union*—an anti-Lincoln paper—has this account: "We pass over the silly remarks of the President; for the credit of the nation we are willing that the veil of oblivion shall be dropped over them and that they shall no more be repeated or thought of."

The *London Times* is harder to categorize. Sometimes the *Times* will run a complimentary article about Lincoln. But generally it adopts the patronizing tone of many of its readers who identify with aristocratic cotton-plantation owners. Here's the *London*

Times account: "[T]he ceremony was rendered ludicrous by some of the sallies of that poor President Lincoln...Anything more dull and commonplace it would not be easy to produce."

What about the Emancipation Address? Today, virtually everyone thinks that emancipating the slaves was a good thing.

But not then. You can predict the response in the South. It is outrage, horror.

But what reaction would you expect in Chicago? Again, consider the source. Here's the way the anti-Lincoln *Chicago Times* greets the Emancipation Proclamation: "We protest against the proclamation, in the name of the Constitution, in behalf of good faith to the conservative millions of the northern and border States... We protest against it as a monstrous usurpation, a criminal wrong, and an act of national suicide."

That was 1862. What about now?

Osama bin Laden has been killed just before the tenth anniversary of 9/11. *The Sandy Springs Neighbor,* A suburban newspaper in Georgia, runs a column with the headline, "Thank You Mr. President."

The writer of the column, Randy Evans, is a staunch Republican—a former General Counsel of the Republican Party of Georgia so it's encouraging to see such fulsome praise for President Obama and the daring raid in Pakistan. But there's a surprise.

The president that the columnist praises is not Barack Obama. It's George W. Bush. The columnist praises Bush because Bush vowed to get Osama bin Laden, even though he didn't. President Obama is not mentioned in the article.

A car with a bumper sticker drives by: "I Do Not Believe the Liberal Media." Now think about that. This driver doesn't believe CNN, CBS, ABC, NBC, MSNBC, *The New York Times*, or *The Washington Post*. That's a lot of information *not* to believe. Anyone who's ever written for those newspapers or had anything to do with those networks knows how much fact-checking goes on.

Just who is the man with the bumper sticker? Is he a member of the Flat Earth Society, or the Tea Party, on his way to a rally, or a Klansman headed to a cross-burning? None of these organizations have high regard from the mainstream media. Or is he just a nice person who's made up his mind, and doesn't want to trouble himself with information that might upset him?

He could just as well have chosen from thousands of other bumper stickers, like "Jesus Saves" or "My grandson is an honor student." But our bumper-sticker guy has selected this message—"I Do Not Believe the Liberal media"—above all others.

A sociologist tells me that this kind of behavior is typical of people who are members of cults.

I get an email that's been forwarded to me. Forwarding emails seems to be a vibrant cottage industry of the far right. The subject line reads, "This photograph says it all."

The photograph shows President Obama standing in front of an American flag with his hands at his side. The people around him have their right hand on their heart. "The Star Spangled Banner" is being played.

I check out the photo at Snopes.com. Snopes.com says the photo is genuine. Obama has explained he is doing what his grandfather taught him to do. You put your hand over your heart when you recite the Pledge of Allegiance; you stand at attention when the national anthem is played. But it's optional.

The Atlanta Braves are playing the LA Dodgers. The national anthem is being sung. I look around me. A man next to me has his hand on his heart. But others are just standing in a more or less alert stance. Some are singing along. A few are holding their phones up to get a photo of the woman singing. If putting your hand on your heart is a test of patriotism, there are lots of unpatriotic people around me.

A man in his sixties at an antique car show in Nebraska is telling me what he thinks about Obama. "I despise the man," he says. He tells me he despises the president because Obama has nationalized health care. One result is there are no emergency rooms in all of Southern California. He read it in an email or on a blog somewhere.

I ask him if he really believes there are no emergency rooms at any hospital in Los Angeles or San Diego. The man stands his ground. "That's what I understand," he replies. He's willing to bet me he's right. I don't take the bet. Seems too much like stealing.

It's April 2012. The Republican primaries are being fought out. Former Senator Santorum is the front-runner. At a rally, he makes this statement, "I was just reading something last night from the state of California. The California universities—I think it's seven or eight of the California system of universities—don't even teach an American history course. It's not even available to be taught."

An easy Google search shows that American history is taught at *every* college and university in the California system, even at its medical college.

But the question arises, where do these people find this stuff?

You can dismiss the meanderings of an old man who fancies antique cars. But it's more difficult to ignore false statements made by a former US Senator who should know better.

Rick Santorum is entitled to his own opinions, but not his own facts.

Is there an honest-to-God, informed resource where people can find the facts?

Actually there are several—Snopes.com and MediaMatters.com—but many people on the right don't trust them.

Enter Politifact, a project which aims to please the right and the left by fact-checking political statements.

Sometimes Politifact is good at it. When it's good, it's very, very good. It wins awards. Even wins the Pulitzer.

But when it's bad? Oh, my!

Here's one about Obama. Obama makes this statement, "Women (are) paid 77 cents on the dollar for doing the same work as men."

Politifact acknowledges that the US Census does report that in 2010, women working full-time earned 77 cents for every dollar earned by men working full-time.

Politifact goes into a long dissertation about outside factors, such as men work in higher paying occupations, etc.

The White House responds to Politifact: "No matter how you look at it, women make less than men—at the same job, at different jobs, weekly, annually, and by occupation."

Politifact acknowledges that the White House is correct: "Nothing in our analysis suggests that gender discrimination doesn't exist. In fact, the experts we consulted agreed that no matter how much you adjust the models to equalize for outside factors, a difference in pay between men and women remains, and it's one that can't be explained away."

Politifact agrees with the experts. You expect the lowest rating the Truth-O-Meter could possibly be is "Almost correct."

But you would be wrong.

The Truth-O-Meter reads "Mostly False."

Maybe they have a rule that the person who sets the Truth-O-Meter is not allowed to read the commentary.

Here's one more Truth-O-Meter story about Obama. It reads, "GOP keeps Guantanamo pledge" and rates it "promise kept."

Obama pledges that he will close Guantanamo within a year. He says Guantanamo hurts the American image abroad, helps al-Qaeda recruit terrorists. He reminds people that nobody has ever escaped from an American maximum-security prison. So, why not bring the prisoners to an American maximum-security prison? In fact, there's a maximum-security prison in Michigan that is closing because of budget cuts. Local people offer it to the government.

But Republicans in Congress vow not to let this happen. They engage in legislative maneuvers that prevent transporting the prisoners from Guantanamo to Michigan or anywhere else in the US.

Scores of men are still in Guantanamo without a trial, or any hope of one.

It is true that Republicans did prevent Obama from keeping his promise by keeping theirs. Politifact calls it a promise kept, and they did keep their promise.

But isn't that like saying that somebody who promises you won't have the highest bid at an auction, and then steals your wallet so you can't make a bid, has kept his promise?

Maybe it doesn't matter all that much what fact-checkers say. Social scientists know that facts have little effect on some people. They will hate what Lincoln or Obama do regardless of the facts.

Communication researchers call it the selective processes: Massive evidence shows that you will try to avoid exposing yourself to messages that you strongly disagree with—*selective exposure*; and, you will forget it quickly if you do—*selective retention*; and, you will interpret it to fit your biases—*selective perception*.

Jonathan Haidt, in *The Righteous Mind,* explains why. It's team behavior. We believe what our team believes in part because of our evolutionary past.

Wolves that hunt in packs and fish that swim in schools have a better survival rate than loners. There still are loners, but loners may not do as well, and the gene pool is affected.

Haidt explains to a reporter, "Once group loyalties are engaged, you can't change people's minds by utterly refuting their arguments. Thinking is mostly just rationalization."

Let's speculate just a bit. If you're hard-wired to be a pack-runner, you probably believe what the pack—your team—believes. And you will rationalize every message you receive that doesn't square with your team's beliefs.

CONCLUSION

I do not pretend to understand the moral universe; the arc is a long one, my eye reaches but little ways; I cannot calculate the curve and complete the figure by the experience of sight, I can divine it by conscience. And from what I see I am sure it bends towards justice.

– Rev. Theodore Parker

CONCLUSION

It would be hard to find a worse time in American history than the 1860s. The nation is being ripped apart. Vicious words have turned into bloody deeds. Yankees and rebels are slaughtering one another by the thousands. It seems probable that government of the people, by the people, for the people, just might perish from the earth.

But the test of a people, and of presidents, is what they do in bad times.

When Lincoln takes the oath of office, one in twelve Americans is a slave. American churches overwhelmingly accept slavery as an institution sanctioned by sacred Scripture. Slaves do not vote. Neither do women. All this in a nation that likens itself to a city set on a hill.

The irony, the hypocrisy of it, is not lost on Lincoln. He issues the Emancipation Proclamation, but it is incomplete and impermanent. A war measure. He pushes through the13th Amendment that ends slavery everywhere in America forever. But he is not done yet.

In the last speech Lincoln ever makes, he proposes that educated black men who've fought for the Union be allowed to vote. That very modest proposal is considered so extreme at the time that John Wilkes Booth, who hears the speech, re-doubles his commitment to kill him.

Who then would have predicted that 150 years later, a black lawyer-politician from Illinois would follow Lincoln's path to the White House?

In a way, what Obama did is not unlike what Roger Bannister did when he broke the four-minute mile. And what Edmund Hillary did when he climbed Mt. Everest. It does not matter how or why or what their motives were. The main thing is, they did it.

And after they did it, others followed. The four-minute mile, which physicians once said is humanly impossible, has been run some 1,200 times since. And over 3,000 individuals have climbed Mt. Everest.

Bannister and Hillary broke mental barriers.

If Obama does nothing else the rest of his life, he will have fame that will endure because of the barrier he broke. He did not just barely break it. Obama got more votes than any candidate in American history.

When it happened, many understood its importance. This night candles were lit at the graveside of Martin Luther King, Jr.

Why is Lincoln revered above all presidents? Here is an answer. When people consider his utter lack of advantages, his slow start, his many setbacks, they think, if he could do it, so can I.

This happens when people break barriers. A man tells me what happened at his Catholic school when JFK was elected. I was just a boy, he says, but his election meant everything to us. We knew that we could dream of being president too. Pictures of JFK were put up on everybody's walls.

And because of Barack Obama, boys and girls who might once have thought the highest office in the land is beyond their reach can now say, "If he did it, so can I."

MY HEARTFELT THANKS TO...

Alice Licht, who was the first one to say to me, "Why don't you write that book?" And then there were kind and supremely talented individuals who edited my words, listened to me read them, provided technical and artistic assistance, advised me what to say and what not to say, fact-checked my assertions, gave me ideas, and offered encouragement: Robin Quinn; Ahmad Meradji; Tom Nixon; Wayne Temple; Donovin Freeman; Gloria Patrnak; Miro Pastrnak; Katrina Dinkle; Juliana Dinkle; Chloe Dinkle; Dylan Griessman; Amelia Davis; Austin McGonigle; Ken Futch; Josh Rahn; Megan Peterson; Angela DeCaires; Caroline Donahue; Rene Godefroy; Bob Chesney; Kenneth Davis; T.W. Hawley; Joan Taub; and Bob English.

QUOTATIONS FROM THE TWO PRESIDENTS

Lincoln

"I'll study and get ready, and then the chance will come."

"You must not wait to be brought forward by the older men...Do you suppose that I should ever have got into notice if I had waited to be hunted up and pushed forward by older men?"

"Always bear in mind that your own resolution to succeed is more important than any other one thing."

"By all means, do not say 'If I can'; say 'I will.'"

"The mode is very simple, though laborious and tedious. It is only to get the books, and read, and study them carefully...Work, work, work is the main thing."

"The leading rule for the lawyer, as for the man of every calling, is diligence. Leave nothing for to-morrow, which can be done to-day."

"I have an irrepressible desire to live till I can be assured that the world is a little better for my having lived in it."

"Neither let us be slandered from our duty by false accusations against us, nor frightened from it by menaces of destruction to the Government, nor of dungeons to ourselves. Let us have faith that right makes might; and in that faith, let us, to the end, dare to do our duty, as we understand it."

"This good earth is plenty broad enough for white man and Negro both, and there is no need of either pushing the other off."

"I claim not to have controlled events, but confess plainly that events have controlled me."

"Twenty-five years ago I was a hired laborer. The hired laborer of yesterday labors on his own account today, and will hire others to labor for him tomorrow. Advancement —improvement in condition—is the order of things in the society of equals."

"If the end brings me out all right, what is said against me won't amount to anything. If the end brings me out wrong, ten angels swearing I was right would make no difference."

Obama

"The best way to not feel hopeless is to get up and do something. Don't wait for good things to happen to you. If you go out and make some good things happen, you will fill the world with hope, you will fill yourself with hope."

"I will never forget that the only reason I'm standing here today is because somebody, somewhere stood up for me when it was risky."

"Making your mark on the world is hard. If it were easy, everybody would do it. But it's not. It takes patience, it takes commitment, and it comes with plenty of failure along the way. The real test is not whether you avoid this failure, because you won't. It's whether you let it harden or shame you into inaction, or whether you learn from it; whether you choose to persevere."

"YES WE CAN!" – Campaign Slogan 2008

"Change will not come if we wait for some other person, or if we wait for some other time. We are the ones we've been waiting for. We are the change that we seek."

"All of us share this world for but a brief moment in time. The question is whether we spend that time focused on what pushes us apart or whether we commit ourselves to an effort, a sustained effort to find common ground, to focus on the future we seek for our children and to respect the dignity of all human beings."

"Our stories may be singular, but our destination is shared."

"There is not a Liberal America and a Conservative America—there is the United States of America."

"Focusing your life solely on making a buck shows a certain poverty of ambition. It asks too little of yourself. Because it's only when you hitch your wagon to something larger than yourself that you realize your true potential."

"It was the labor movement that helped secure so much of what we take for granted today. The forty-hour work week, the minimum wage, family leave, health insurance, Social Security, Medicare, retirement plans. The cornerstones of the middle-class security all bear the union label."

"One of the things I think you understand as president is you're held responsible for everything, but you don't always have control of everything."

"We lose ourselves when we compromise the very ideals that we fight to defend. And we honor those ideals by upholding them not when it's easy, but when it is hard."

"America is a land of big dreamers and big hopes. It is this hope that has sustained us through revolution and civil war, depression and world war, a struggle for civil and social rights, and the brink of nuclear crisis. And it is because our dreamers dreamed that we have emerged from each challenge more united, more prosperous, and more admired than before."

"For all the cruelty and hardship of our world, we are not mere prisoners of fate. Our actions matter and can bend history in the direction of justice."

"We the people, declare today that the most evident of truths— that all of us are created equal—is the star that guides us still; just as it guided our forebears through Seneca Falls, and Selma, and Stonewall; just as it guided all those men and women, sung and unsung, who left footprints along this great Mall, to hear a preacher say that we cannot walk alone; to hear a King proclaim that our individual freedom is inextricably bound to the freedom of every soul on Earth."

INDEX

ABOUT THE AUTHOR

Dr. Gene Griessman is internationally known for his presentations on change, leadership, and communication. He has spoken at conventions and annual meetings and has conducted seminars all over the world. As actor and playwright, he has performed his one-man play on Abraham Lincoln at Ford's Theatre, the Georgia Dome, the Ice Palace, the Lincoln Memorial, and aboard the famed carrier, the USS *Abraham Lincoln*. He has conducted exclusive interviews with US Presidents, famous actors, sports figures, business leaders, and Nobel Laureates.

Winner of the Benjamin Franklin Award and the Kay Herman Legacy Award, he often appears on television and radio, and his award-winning productions have aired on WCNN and TBS.

Dr. Griessman has taught at the College of William and Mary, North Carolina State University, Auburn University, Tuskegee Universtiy, and Georgia Tech. He has served as Fulbright professor at Quaid-i-Azam University (the national graduate university of Pakistan) and as visiting researcher at the University of New South Wales in Australia.

He has been listed in *Who's Who in America* and *Who's Who in the World*. He is a voting member of the Television Academy of Arts and Sciences.

WATCH GENE GRIESSMAN
www.presidentlincoln.com

TWITTER
@lincolnandobama

WEBSITES
www.lincolnandobama.com
www.whatyousay.com

BOOK GENE GRIESSMAN:
www.presidentlincoln.com
www.atlantaspeakersbureau.com
abe@mindspring.com
404.256.5927

FOR QUANTITY ORDERS AND PROMOTIONS:
abe@mindspring.com
404.256.5927

COMING SOON

GENE GRIESSMAN'S NEWEST BOOK

GREAT COACHES: WHAT YOU CAN LEARN FROM THEM